Marian Cox

Cambridge Checkpoint
English

Coursebook

8

CAMBRIDGE
UNIVERSITY PRESS

CAMBRIDGE
UNIVERSITY PRESS

University Printing House, Cambridge CB2 8BS, United Kingdom

One Liberty Plaza, 20th Floor, New York, NY 10006, USA

477 Williamstown Road, Port Melbourne, VIC 3207, Australia

314–321, 3rd Floor, Plot 3, Splendor Forum, Jasola District Centre, New Delhi – 110025, India

79 Anson Road, #06–04/06, Singapore 079906

Cambridge University Press is part of the University of Cambridge.

It furthers the University's mission by disseminating knowledge in the pursuit of education, learning and research at the highest international levels of excellence.

www.cambridge.org
Information on this title: www.cambridge.org/9781107690998

First published 2013

40 39 38 37 36 35 34 33 32 31 30 29 28 27 26 25 24 23

Printed in Dubai by Oriental Press

A catalogue record for this publication is available from the British Library

ISBN 978-1-107-69099-8 Paperback

Contents

Introduction

Welcome to Cambridge Checkpoint English Stage 8.

The Cambridge Checkpoint English course covers the Cambridge Secondary 1 English framework and is divided into three stages: 7, 8 and 9. This book covers all you need to know for stage 8.

There are two more books in the series to cover stages 7 and 9, which have a different focus. Together they will give you a firm foundation in English.

At the end of the year, your teacher may ask you to take a **Progression test** to find out how well you have done. This book will help you to learn how to apply your knowledge of language and your skills in reading and writing in order to do well in the test. At the end of stage 9, you will be asked to do a **Checkpoint test** to find out how much you have learnt over all three stages.

The framework's focus for stage 8 is **Description and information**, and the study of accounts and short stories. The curriculum is presented in fiction and non-fiction content areas, and the skills are divided into Language (phonics, spelling and vocabulary, grammar and punctuation), Reading, Writing, and Speaking and Listening. There is no assessment of Speaking and Listening in the Progression tests or the Checkpoint test, but these skills, practised as individual, pair, group and class activities, are developed in all the units.

The topic for this book is **Wider world**. The content is about time and place, people and the things they do.

This book has 12 units, each of which is a mixture of fiction and non-fiction passages and activities. There are no clear dividing lines between language and literature, or between reading and writing skills. Skills learnt in one unit are often used in other units. There is, however, some progression in the order in which the skills are introduced, and how you will be revisiting the skills practised in stage 7.

Each unit starts with an introduction which will prepare you for what you will learn in the unit, and a starter activity to get you thinking and talking. Each unit contains several kinds of passage and asks you to practise several skills. **Key points** explain rules and give information about aspects of reading and writing. **Tip** boxes provide help with specific activities. The activities are separated into stages to give you support. At the end of each unit you will be asked to do a piece of extended writing to give you the opportunity to practise the kind of writing you will be asked to do in the Checkpoint test. Other kinds of writing will be included in the activities. You will also practise reading the kinds of passage which are included in the Checkpoint test, and learn to read closely so that you notice the details of the content and of the language.

There are many different types of verse and prose in this book, and your knowledge of literature will be developed as well as your language skills. You will discuss ideas and methods with other students as well as with your teacher. These discussions are an important part of developing your language skills and understanding of literature. The contents list on page iii tells you what kinds of reading passage and writing activities are in each unit.

We hope the course will be enjoyable and will help you to feel confident about responding to and using English in a variety of ways.

UNIT 1 Fire

This unit focuses on descriptive accounts. You will practise identifying and using precise and evocative vocabulary and images, and selecting, paraphrasing and sequencing notes for informative purposes. You will also learn more about past participles, connectives, the role of adverbs, and the use of *would* for repeated action in the past.

Activities

1 **a** Tell a partner how you feel about fire, and about incidents you can remember in your life where fire was involved (e.g. when you were kept warm by a fire indoors or outdoors).

b Contribute to a word cloud to be collected on the board of all the words which relate to the idea of fire, with both positive and negative connotations. Think of all the different kinds of fire there are (e.g. matches, lightning) as well as adjectives used to describe it.

c Collect a list on the board of stories, novels and films in which fire plays an important role. Discuss the role of fire and what it represents in each case.

2 There are many proverbs which use fire as their image. Work with a partner on the following activities.

a Paraphrase these proverbs.
i Out of the frying pan into the fire.
ii There's no smoke without fire.
iii One should fight fire with fire.
iv Fire is a good servant but a bad master.
v Don't start a fire you can't put out.

b Research or remember other proverbs and sayings about fire, and share them with the class. Some may be local to your country.

c Look at the photograph on the previous page of an Amazonian forest fire.
i Write down all the words, phrases and images which come to mind as you look at it.
ii Now asterisk the more interesting and memorable ones, and think of reasons why they are more powerful than the others.
iii Share your asterisked choices with the rest of the class.

Text 1A is Pliny the Younger's description in a letter of the eruption of Mount Vesuvius at Pompeii, western Italy, in AD 79.

Text 1A

On 24th August, in the early afternoon, a cloud appeared over the Bay of Naples. The general appearance of the cloud rising from the mountain can best be expressed as being like an umbrella pine, for it rose to a great height on a kind of trunk and then split off into branches. In places it looked white, elsewhere blotched and dirty, according to the amount of soil and ashes it carried with it.

Later, ashes were falling, hotter and thicker as ships drew near, followed by bits of pumice and blackened stones, **charred** and cracked by the flames; then suddenly the ships were in shallow water, and the shore was blocked by the **debris** from the mountain.

Meanwhile, on Mount Vesuvius, broad sheets of fire and leaping flames blazed at several points, their bright glare **emphasised** by the darkness of the night. The buildings were now shaking with violent shocks, and seemed to be swaying to and fro as if they had been torn from their foundations. Carriages began to run in different directions though the ground was quite level, and would not remain **stationary** even when wedged with stones. We also saw the sea sucked away and apparently forced back by the earthquake: at any rate it **receded** from the shore so that quantities of sea creatures were left stranded on dry sand. On the landward side a fearful black cloud was rent by forked and quivering bursts of flame, and parted to reveal great tongues of fire, like flashes of lightning magnified in size.

Soon afterwards the cloud sank down to earth and covered the sea, spreading over the earth like a flood, as if the universe had been plunged into eternal darkness for evermore.

At last the darkness thinned and dispersed like smoke or cloud; then there was daylight, but yellowish as it is during an eclipse. Everything was changed, buried deep in ashes like snowdrifts.

3 In this activity you will look more closely at the vocabulary in Text 1A.

a Pick out the words and phrases which you think are most strongly descriptive in Text 1A. Explain why you think they are so powerful and memorable.

b Give synonyms for the five words in bold in Text 1A. Are they as effective as the original words, and if not, why?

    charred   debris   emphasised   stationary   receded

c The five bold words in the passage are difficult to spell. Write them out, along with the other five words below, with their 'hot spots' underlined. Then write them three times each without looking at the word. After that you can check to see if you were right.

    appearance   apparently   quantities   creatures   tongues

4　**a** Imagine that you witnessed the scene described in Text 1A. Write notes which record the main features. Use your own words as far as possible and avoid figurative language.

   b Now imagine you are a news reporter for the *Pompeii Times*. Interview your partner about what they witnessed of the eruption, and make notes of what they say as the basis of your report. Include direct speech to use as a quotation from the witness.

   c Write your news report, of about one page, after you have ordered the notes into an appropriate sequence. Use the key point below to help you. Begin your report 'Yesterday evening . . .' and remember to include a headline and one subheading in the middle of the report. When you have finished, swap reports with your partner to check for errors, then give it to your teacher.

Key point

News reports

Style:
- The aim of a news report is to be as informative as possible, so names, ages and exact dates and numbers are given, in a condensed way: for example, 'Neighbour and ex-employee, Imraan Patel, 35, rang the fire brigade.'
- Because of a need to save space, the headline is as short as possible, not only in overall length (usually no more than five words) but also in the length of the individual words (monosyllables where possible, e.g. *bid, plan, break*).
- Beyond the number ten, numbers are used instead of words in journalistic writing.
- Present rather than past tense verbs are used in headlines and elsewhere to save space and to make the events seem more dramatic.
- Since the aim of news reports is informative, figurative language is not appropriate.
- A subheading, which is a short phrase, sometimes taken from an interview to follow, keeps up the reader's interest in what is to come.

Structure:
- The structure of a news report is different from that of other kinds of writing because it starts with what happened most recently, usually yesterday.

- In the first couple of paragraphs, it gives the basic information – the who, what, when and where: for example, 'Late last night there was a serious fire at the SuperComfy furniture warehouse on the outskirts of New Delhi.'
- It goes on to give the background to the news event: for example, 'Only recently a safety inspection by the regional Fire Department found that the alarm and sprinkler systems were not up to standard.'
- It may then interview a witness or someone affected by the event (e.g. the owner of the warehouse or of a nearby endangered property). Their comments may be included as direct speech to give drama and variety to the report.
- Finally, a news item will say what is currently happening (e.g. that the fire is still smouldering or that firefighters are searching the ashes for clues to the cause of the fire) or give a prediction for the future (e.g. that there will be an inquiry into the incident in two weeks' time or that the owners have said that the fire was deliberately started by a business rival and that this will be proved). So instead of a chronological structure, a news report goes from recent past → past (or further past) → present → future.
- You may not be able to use all of the available information and may have to select what is most important for the reader to know.

Text 1B

All that is _____ does not glitter,
   Not all those who wander are _____ :
The old that is strong does not wither,
   Deep roots are not _____ by the frost.

From the _____ a fire shall be woken,
   A light from the shadows shall _____ :
Renewed shall be _____ that was broken,
   The _____ again shall be king.

From The Fellowship of the Ring *by J.R.R. Tolkien*

5 Work on Text 1B in small groups.

a Fill in the missing words on a copy of the poem. To help you, pay attention to the rhyme and metre, and the use of alliteration, assonance and antithesis (contrast).

b On a copy of the poem put this symbol ´ above the syllables which are stressed. Then look at the rhyming words. What can you say about the rhyme scheme and metre of the poem?

c Paraphrase in your own words the message of the poem.

d Think of a title for the poem.

e Write another four-line verse for the poem, in the same form. It must continue the same idea.

Text 1C is an extract from an informative book which describes watching a steam train pass.

Text 1C

Every night, at exactly eight minutes past nine, it <u>roars</u> through the village. I can see it coming several miles away, its powerful headlight <u>fingering</u> rails and telegraph wires with a shimmer of light. Silently and slowly it seems to draw nearer; then suddenly, it is almost above me. A wild roar of steam and driving wheels, the wail of its hoarse whistle at the crossing, and then, <u>looming</u> black against the night sky, it <u>smashes</u> past, and in the swing of drivers and connecting rods I think of a greyhound, or a racehorse <u>thundering</u> the final stretch. High in the cab window, a motionless figure peers ahead into the night; suddenly he is blackly <u>silhouetted</u> by the glare of the opened fire-door, and in the orange light I can see the fireman swing back and forth as he <u>feeds</u> his fire. The light <u>burns</u> against the flying steam

and smoke above; then blackness – and now the white windows of the carriages <u>flicker</u> past, and through the swirl of dust and smoke I watch the two red lights <u>sink</u> down the track.

From America at Work *by Joseph Husband*

6   **a**   Look at the ten underlined figurative verbs in Text 1C. Explain in your notebook what effect each one creates and why it is appropriate.

     b   Explain, in detail, how the device of antithesis is being used in this text.

     c   Explain, with examples, the effect of the alliteration in the text.

7   **a**   On a copy of Text 1C, put brackets ( ) in pencil around the adverbs.

     b   Read the key point on the role of adverbs. Then discuss with a partner which adverbs can be removed from Text 1C without loss of meaning. Erase the brackets if you think the adverb is adding something extra to the description.

     c   Decide with a partner the places in the passage where adverbs could be inserted to give additional meaning, and what the adverbs would be.

Key point

Role of adverbs

Often adverbs are used in a lazy way, that is to say that they are tacked onto a weak verb and the description is less powerful than if a stronger and more precise verb had been selected, making the adverb unnecessary. Unless the adverb is adding something new to the meaning, they are better not used, especially if they have been used already in the same passage.

    In good descriptive writing the effectiveness of the description is due to the choice of interesting and unusual verbs and adjectives, and the images they form. Adverbs are a kind of telling but not showing: for example, 'He threw the ball violently' is weaker than 'He hurled the ball'; 'She left the room quickly' is not as effective as 'She fled the room', which has connotations of terror as well as speed.

Text 1D is adapted from a *Sunday Times* magazine article about how in ancient times warships were set alight by mirrors.

ARCHIMEDES' SECRET DEATH RAY

For the Romans it looked like their easiest battle. They came to invade Syracuse – and found soldiers with mirrors.

As their boats approached the coast of Sicily the sun came out, a light beam leapt from the shore and their boats burst into flames. They had become victims of the first 'death ray'.

For centuries **archeologists** have argued over descriptions of how Archimedes, antiquity's greatest inventor, used **concentrated** solar energy to destroy the Roman fleet in 212 BC.

Historians have said nobody then knew enough about optics and mirrors. This month, however, a study will show that some ancient **civilisations**, including that of the Ancient Greeks, had such advanced scientific knowledge that they may even have made telescopes – an invention attributed to the 16th-century **astronomer** Galileo – and that 'burning mirrors' would have been within their reach.

Archimedes, a Greek born around 280 BC, was famed for his mathematical skills and his ability to use them for building war machines. These included catapults that hurled boulders at the enemy, long chutes that could be projected from the city walls for rocks to be rolled down, and cranes with grappling hooks that could lift ships and shake the sailors into the water.

Archimedes is best known for running through Syracuse shouting 'Eureka' after realising, while in the bath, that he could work out the purity of gold by measuring the volume of water it displaced. For his fellow citizens, however, that would have been trivial compared with a death ray for **incinerating** the dreaded Romans.

There were later examples of the use of the death ray, the first being in 6th-century Constantinople; when the Byzantine capital was besieged by enemy ships, dozens of men holding mirrors set fire to them.

Modern scientists have recreated such events under controlled conditions. In 1973 a Greek scientist lined up 60 sailors on a quay with large mirrors, from which they reflected light onto a small boat 50 metres away. The boat was in flames within three minutes.

8 Complete in your notebook these sentences about Text 1D.

a Archimedes was
 i Roman ii Sicilian iii Greek.

b Archimedes was alive in
 i 212 BC ii the 16th century iii the 6th century.

c Archimedes lived in
 i Sicily ii Italy iii Constantinople.

d Archimedes was
 i an historian ii a mathematician iii an archeologist.

e Archimedes invented
 i gold ii burning mirrors iii warships.

The following activities focus on the vocabulary and grammar of Text 1D.

9 a Write definitions for the words in bold in Text 1D, as they are used in the passage. Then check your definitions in a dictionary.

archeologists concentrated civilisations
astronomer incinerating

b Write your own sentences including each of these words, demonstrating that you understand their meaning.

c With a partner, list in three columns all the words you can think of which contain the following letter strings:

 i *scop* or *optic*, which mean vision

 ii *ology*, which means study

 iii *scienc/t*, which means knowledge.

10 a On a copy of Text 1D, underline the uses of the present perfect tense (e.g. 'they have said'). Give the rule for how the tense is formed.

b Look at the final paragraph of the passage. Why is the first verb in the present perfect tense when the others are in the past simple? Discuss with a partner the rule for using the present perfect tense. Give two examples of your own of sentences which contain verbs in both the past simple and present perfect.

c The second part of the verb in the present perfect tense is called the past participle. Circle five irregular past participles in Text 1D.

Key point

Past participles

Regular past participles end in *-ed*, e.g. *walked*. However, strong/ irregular verbs in English have irregular past participles, just as they also have irregular past simple forms (e.g. *bring → brought → brought; sing → sang → sung*). Sometimes the form is the same for the past simple and the past participle. These have to be learnt, which is not difficult as they are the most commonly used verbs. Some have optional forms, one older and one more recent (e.g. *burned/burnt; leaped/leapt*). They may not be pronounced the way they are spelt (e.g. *read → read*).

We use the present perfect for a recent action, or one with no time specified or implied, or one which is not yet completed: for example, 'I have looked for it everywhere but I haven't found it yet.' The time adverbs *yet, just* or *since* are often used with the present perfect. The past participle, with *had* instead of *have*, is also used to form the past perfect tense. This tense refers to actions which happened further back in the past than the past simple, or to the order in which events happened in the past: for example, 'I had arrived home before I remembered that I had left my bag at school.'

Greek myth: The Gift of Fire

Prometheus was a Titan, one of the old gods. His father, Iapetus, led a revolt against Zeus, the chief of the new race of gods. Prometheus felt sorry for newly created humans, who had to live on the cold earth, and wanted to give fire to them. Zeus forbade this, and guarded the entrance to Olympus, the mountain home of the gods, so that Prometheus could not steal it. But the goddess Athena told him of a back entrance, so Prometheus was able to steal fire and smuggle it to humans. Zeus was very angry that Prometheus had disobeyed him, so he ordered that Prometheus be chained to a rock. Every day a great eagle would come to Prometheus and eat his liver, leaving only at nightfall, when the liver would begin to grow back once more. At daybreak, the eagle would return to the chained Prometheus and again attack his liver. The daily ritual would be repeated for ever.

Cherokee myth: The First Fire

Every animal that could fly or swim was anxious to go and collect fire from the hollow sycamore tree on an island. The Raven, who was very confident, was sent first. He flew high and far across the water and alighted on the tree. While he was wondering what to do next, the heat scorched all his feathers black, as they are to this day. He was scared and went back without the fire.

The Screech Owl volunteered to go next and reached the place safely. While he was looking down into the hollow tree, a blast of hot air came up and nearly burned out his eyes. He just managed to fly home, but it was a long time before he could see well, and his eyes are red to this day.

No more of the birds would venture, and so the Racer Snake said he would go through the water and bring back the fire. He swam across to the island and crawled through the grass to the tree, and entered it through a small hole at the bottom. The heat and the smoke were too much for him too, and his body was charred black, as it still is to this day.

The animals held another council, because there was still no fire and the world was cold, but birds, snakes and four-footed animals all had some excuse for not going because they were all afraid of the burning sycamore, until at last the Water Spider said she would go. But the question was, 'How could you bring back the fire?' Water Spider said, 'I'll manage.' She crossed over to the island and through the grass to the fiery tree. She put one small burning coal into a bowl attached to her back with her own thread, and returned with it, and ever since we have had fire.

 a Discuss in class:
- the role of myths in a culture
- the definition of a myth
- the difference between a myth and a legend.

b i Which of the fire myths, Texts 1E and 1F, do you prefer? Take a vote in class.

 ii Discuss how the differences in style, as well as in content, have influenced your preference.

c On a copy of Text 1E, underline the use of *would* in the last three sentences. How is it being used? How does it compare with the use of *would* in the first sentence of the penultimate (last but one) paragraph of Text 1F?

d On a copy of Text 1F, underline the subordinate clauses in the complex sentences, i.e. those which have a finite verb form but are dependent on the main clause of the sentence (e.g. '<u>because</u> they *were* all afraid of the burning sycamore').

e Rewrite the story of Prometheus in Text 1E in complex sentences. You may change the order of the information if necessary. Read the key point below to help you.

Key point

More complex connectives

Remember that sentences which use the connectives *and*, *but*, *so* and *or* to link simple sentences are called compound sentences, which means that both parts are equal and could exist on their own: for example, 'The cat sat on the mat and it went to sleep.'

However, this is not the best way to construct sentences because they are monotonous and do not convey complex ideas or the relationship between events. The story in Text 1E does not contain many complex sentences, and that is why it probably seemed less interesting to you than the second myth.

You have already learnt about forming complex sentences in two ways:

- using *if* and *unless*, e.g. 'If he does go, he will not regret it.'
- using the relative pronouns *who* and *which* (and *whose* and *whom*), e.g. 'The fire, which had seemed under control, suddenly became even more fierce.'

You can also use connectives to make complex sentences, such as the following:

before	after	because	as	since	(al)though
when	whenever	where	wherever	while	until

12   **a**   Brainstorm all the words which come into your mind when you think of fireworks. Think about all of the five senses.

      b   Turn some of your words into images (e.g. 'rockets are launched to the stars'; 'sparklers splash liquid gold'; 'broken necklaces shed pearls of light'). Consider sounds as well as meanings.

      c   Using your images:
         i   write an acrostic poem on the word FIREWORKS
        ii   write a shape poem called 'Fireworks'.

13   Working in small groups, produce a leaflet about firework safety or lighting a fire outdoors.

      a   Organise in two columns your collective ideas about the hazards involved and what can be done to reduce them (e.g. 'pets get frightened – keep them indoors with windows closed'; 'grass may be dry – choose a patch of earth where there is no grass'). Think about where, when and how fires or fireworks should be lit and by whom.

b Design a draft of a leaflet which contains a numbered list of between six and ten safety instructions. Think about suitable illustrations and decide on the leaflet heading (e.g. 'Better safe than sorry'; 'Fire can kill').

c Produce your leaflet, which can be done using a computer design program and clip art or visual software. The group members should agree on the language accuracy, the overall design of the leaflet, the positioning and order of the text, the graphics and the colour scheme. It can then be displayed in your classroom, along with your firework poems.

Key point

Leaflets

Leaflets are purely informative texts and they need to be simple in expression and layout.

- Numbers and bullet points are often used, and sometimes subheadings and boxes draw attention to key ideas.
- Illustrations need to be in bright, eye-catching colours.
- Key words should be capitalised, underlined, in bold or in a larger size.
- Instructions are expressed in the imperative verb form, often with exclamation marks, to make the message shorter, clearer and more authoritative (e.g. 'Don't stand too close!').
- Rhyme and alliteration can be used to make the advice more memorable: for example, 'On fireworks night, do things right!'; 'Never fool with fire!'

14 You have now learnt a lot about ways of describing fire and are ready to write your own description of a fire of some kind, using ideas from the texts in this unit. You could describe a huge raging inferno, a local building in flames or a fire in a domestic fireplace. The quality of the description – the ability to make the reader feel that they are witnessing it – is what matters.

a Plan your ideas and include phrases you would like to use.

b Decide on the best sequence for your description. Think especially about how to start and how to end it.

c Write out your final version, then check it carefully before giving it in. Check not only for accuracy but to make sure you have avoided repetition and used interesting language.

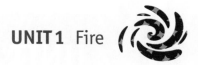

Key point

Descriptive writing

- Using the first person and the present tense gives authority and immediacy to your description, giving the impression that you saw the object or event for yourself and it is happening now.

- Keep a picture of what you are describing in your mind and be very precise and specific in your choice of vocabulary, using exact colours for instance. Put adjectives in front of each noun, avoiding vague and clichéd words such as *lovely* or *horrible*, which do not convey a clear picture.

- Refer to as many of the five senses as you can to create an atmosphere. Description isn't only about what you can see.

- Use figurative language, similes and metaphors to convey the exact picture.

- Use a variety of sentence structures; any kind of repetition can spoil descriptive writing, and that includes the type of sentences you use. It is especially important not to begin every sentence the same way (e.g. with *It* or *The fire*). Remember that you can use *would* to describe repeated actions in the past: for example, 'Every so often, flames would shoot through the branches.'

- Avoid facts and statistics, as this is creative not informative writing. Your description can include your thoughts and feelings to make the reader feel more involved in the experience.

- Provide a framework for your description. This may take the form of a chronological structure, e.g. the duration of the fire, showing how it changes within a short time span; or a spatial structure, i.e. how what you see, hear, etc. develops as the thing you are describing moves towards or away from you, or as you move nearer to or further away from it. The temperature and noise would increase and more details would become visible as you approached a fire.

UNIT 2 Games and sports

This unit looks at informative and instructional writing, including the use of modal verbs and passives. The activities involve constructing and punctuating sentences; selecting, sequencing and editing information; giving a chronological account; writing a diary entry; and giving an informative talk.

Activities

1　**a** Collect on the board in two lists the games and sports played by members of the class.

　　b Decide on the difference between a game and a sport, and define them both.

　　c Discuss the reasons for games and sports and their role in our lives.

Text 2A

The ancient game of backgammon

<u>Referred</u> to by **different** names in different countries – such as *tavli* in Greece, *shan-liu* in China, *takhteh nard* in Iran, and *shesh besh* in Arabic countries – the game of backgammon is an **ancient** one (going back over 5000 years to the Persian empire) which is still played all over the world today.

There was a <u>revival</u> of the game in the 1970s, when the first Backgammon World Championship was held in the Bahamas. Since the 1980s, video games have gradually <u>replaced</u> all types

of board game, **especially** for young people. Typically, it is the older generation which is seen playing backgammon in open-air cafés around the Mediterranean and in the Middle East (and nearly always men).

The game is **immediately** <u>recognisable</u> from the sound of dice being rolled against wood. The board is also distinctive, as it is divided in two with 12 triangles painted in each half of a hinged box – usually made of lacquered wood in different colours of brown – in which the pieces can be stored.

The aim of the game, which is **designed** for two players, is to move one's pieces across the board according to the numbers shown on the dice. It is normally played with 30 'stones' – 15 each, black or white – and two dice, which are thrown **simultaneously**. Pieces are <u>removed</u> once they reach 'home', and the winner is the person who – while at the same time managing to block the moves of their opponent – gets all their pieces home first.

Some believe that it is purely a matter of luck; others claim that one has to be **skilful**. In tournaments **professional competitors** play very quickly, so **experience**, confidence and expertise are then important factors in determining who wins.

2
a Select the five main facts about backgammon, and copy them as phrases into your notebook.

b Reorder them logically and join them together in your own words as complex sentences.

c Find and list the ten examples of the passive verb form in the passage. Why do you think this type of writing uses a lot of passives? Discuss it in class and then read the key point below.

Key point

Passives in informative writing

It is usual to find many passive verb forms in informative writing because it is formal, objective and avoids emphasis on the performers of the verbs. The humans are not relevant and would distract from the necessary focus of the description or instruction. Sometimes the passive is used in instructions because it is more polite, e.g. 'It should be sent' rather than 'You should send it'.

3 **a** Look at the ten words in bold in Text 2A, which are considered difficult to spell. Look up their meanings if you aren't sure. Study their 'hot spots', then cover the words and write them in your notebook. After that, check that you have written them correctly.

i different   iv immediately   vii skilful   ix competitors

ii ancient   v designed   viii professional   x experience

iii especially   vi simultaneously

b Look at the following words from the passage:

referred   revival   replaced   recognisable   removed

They share one of the commonest prefixes in English. Discuss with a partner what you think *re* means, and list five more words you know with the same prefix.

c In pairs, study the uses of the pairs of dashes and brackets in Text 2A. Discuss how they have been used. Then define what you think the rule is for the use of double dashes and brackets in a sentence.

Key point

Parentheses

A parenthesis is a part of a sentence that could be left out because it is grammatically unnecessary and because the information contained within it is extra to the main point being made in the sentence. For example, in the first paragraph of Text 2A we have already been told that the game of backgammon has different names in different parts of the world, so the list between the dashes is just giving some examples but not giving any new information.

You already know that a single dash shows when an extra thought is added to the end of a sentence, and that the use of two commas creates a parenthesis, a piece which can be 'cut out'; now you have a choice of two other ways of creating the same effect.

Whether you use commas, dashes or brackets doesn't really matter, although brackets give the impression that the information contained between them is even less necessary than that contained between commas or dashes, because it seems visually to be more separate from the main idea of the sentence, more 'by the way'.

Where a sentence needs more than one parenthesis it is a good idea to use a mixture of different types. Don't forget that if you open a parenthesis you need to make sure that you close it.

The rules for the board game Snakes (or Chutes) and Ladders

The board is in the form of a grid with ten rows of ten squares. Each player starts with a token on the starting square (the no. 1 square in the bottom left corner of the board) and takes turns to roll a single die to move the token by the number of squares <u>which are</u> indicated by the die roll. Tokens should follow the fixed route <u>which is</u> marked on the game-board, which is a track from the bottom to the top of the playing area, passing once through every square. If, on completion of a move, your token lands on the lower-numbered end of a 'ladder', you should move your token up to the square at the top of the ladder. If you land at the top of a 'snake' (or 'chute'), you should move your token down to the snake's bottom square. If you rolled a 6, you could, after moving, immediately take another turn. If you roll three consecutive 6s, you should return to the starting square, and should not move again until rolling another 6. The player <u>who is</u> first to bring their token to the last square of the track is the winner. It is a game <u>which consists</u> purely of luck, and it could take a long time to get to square 100.

The following activities focus on grammar aspects of Text 2B.

 a Look at the underlined phrases in Text 2B containing *who* and *which*. Discuss with a partner why they do not have a comma before them.

b Try to describe to the class how the examples in the text are different from those below, which *do* have commas:

The game, which consists purely of luck, is very popular.
The player sitting on the left, who was very skilful, managed to win.

c Read the key point on the next page about defining relative clauses. Then write four sentences of your own, two using *who* and two using *which*, both with and without commas before them. Read your sentences to the class to see if they agree with your use of defining and non-defining relative clauses.

Key point

Defining relative clauses

When the clause containing *who* or *which* can be separated from the rest of the sentence, so that what remains would still make sense without it, we show this with a comma. It is called a non-defining relative clause. Sometimes, however, the *who* or *which* cannot be separated from what comes before because it is part of the description and if it were removed, what was left would not make sense. For example, in Text 2B it would not make sense to say in the penultimate sentence that 'The player . . . is the winner', or in the last sentence that 'It is a game . . . and it could take a long time.' We call these non-removable descriptions 'defining' relative clauses because they are part of the definition of the subject: for example, 'A teacher is someone who passes information to students.'

5

  a   Notice how often the personal pronoun 'you' occurs in Text 2B. Share with the class why you think this is.

  b   On a copy of Text 2B, underline the uses of *should* and *could*. Notice how they are used and the difference between them.

  c   Now read the key point below on modal verbs. Think of a board game you know how to play. Write a half-page description of the rules for playing the game. Address the reader as 'you' and use conditional ('if') sentences including *should* and *could*, as in Text 2B.

Key point

Modal verbs

Modals are auxiliary verbs which can be followed directly by main verbs in the infinitive without 'to'. They include the forms of the verbs *have* and *be*. You have learnt about **would**, which is used as the past tense of *will*, for repetitive actions in the past, and in conditional sentences to express something which is possible under certain circumstances (e.g. 'If he worked more hours, he *would* earn more money').

  Could is the past tense of *can*; it is less definite than *would*, but it can also be used to indicate something which is possible, as a suggestion or prediction (e.g. 'He *could* try again later'; 'She *could* do really well in the race').

Should is the past form of *shall*, but it is almost as strong as *must* when it is used in advice and instructions (e.g. 'He *should* leave immediately'; 'They *should* not be afraid').

You can see the difference in strength of these three modal verbs in this sentence: 'I said that I *could* postpone my visit, and that in fact I *would* do so, because I *should* not go there alone.'

 Text 2C

Kung fu nuns

Last week young Buddhist nuns gave demonstrations of their skill at kung fu, a Chinese martial art, to thousands of **pilgrims** attending the Second Annual Drukpa Conference in Nepal.

The Amitabha Drukpa nunnery has revealed that interest in becoming a nun has increased hugely since classes in kung fu have been offered there. Each morning hundreds of devotees walk clockwise around a golden statue of Buddha, while on the roof the nuns practise the same kung fu fighting which was made famous in the 1970s by films starring Bruce Lee, a Hong Kongese actor and martial arts instructor.

The nunnery, belonging to an 800-year-old sect, is on a hillside outside Kathmandu, capital of Nepal. Here the young Buddhist nuns are taught kung fu by a Vietnamese master, who began teaching at the nunnery two years ago. It was introduced into Amitabha Drukpa by the leader of the spiritual sect, His Holiness The Gyalwang Drukpa. Drukpa means *dragon*, and this sect, the main religion of Bhutan, is widely followed across the Himalayan countries.

The Gyalwang Drukpa says that he felt that previous spiritual leaders had not done enough to advance the rights of women. He decided that the introduction of kung fu was the best thing that he could do for them. He got the idea after seeing nuns in Vietnam being taught kung fu. The nuns must practise up to two hours every day.

The nunnery, built by The Gyalwang Drukpa, is modern and well-equipped for worship and study. The sect puts emphasis on the importance of **meditation** and happiness.

One of the nuns, a 16-year-old from India, says that kung fu helps her to concentrate on her prayers and studies. She says, 'Meditation becomes easier after **disciplined** exercise, and it's also good for our health.' Another Indian nun says she likes the fact that kung fu gives her strength and safety. 'It protects us to have this physical power,' she says.

Normally nuns in the Himalayas are seen as **inferior** to monks and are overlooked, so this amount of attention is unusual. They have traditionally been treated as servants, kitchen-workers and gardeners in the monasteries.

A senior Buddhist nun, Jetsunma Tenzin Palmo, who attended the conference, says that she wants to introduce kung fu into her own nunnery in the Indian state of Himachal Pradesh. She says that 'it arouses a sense of self-confidence which is very important for nuns, and it keeps young men in the area away when they know that the nuns are kung fu experts'. She reports that since nunneries have begun to offer better education, and physical programmes like kung fu, the number of girls wanting to become nuns has grown **dramatically**.

6 **a** Write your own words or phrases to explain the meaning of the five words in bold in Text 2C, as they are used in the passage. Try to work out the meanings from the context.

pilgrims   meditation   disciplined   inferior   dramatically

b With a partner, find the nouns in the text which have been formed by adding a suffix to a verb or adjective (e.g. *demonstration*). How many different kinds of noun ending can you find? Look at the key point on the next page to help you.

c Find all the examples in Text 2C of noun phrases in apposition (i.e. in parenthesis). See the tip on the next page if you need help.

Key point

Noun endings

The main noun endings are *ance/ence, ion/action/ation/tion, ety, ness*. Which one is adopted depends on the type of ending of the verb or adjective from which the noun is formed.

The noun endings *er* and *ee* are for people, depending on whether they are active or passive (e.g. *employer, employee*), while *ery* is usually a place ending (e.g. *nunnery, bakery*).

For Activity 6c
Phrases in apposition

A phrase in apposition is one where what is between two commas refers to the same as what came before: for example, 'My next-door neighbour, Suzy Wong, is an excellent cook.' The neighbour and Suzy Wong are the same person. As with all pairs of commas which 'cut out' some extra words, you could remove the phrase in apposition and the sentence would still be complete and correct.

7 Imagine that you were the journalist who wrote the news report in Text 2C, and your editor has asked you to reduce it to about half its length, without losing any of the information.

a   On a copy of the text:
- put a line through any repetition of information
- put square brackets around any descriptive details which you do not consider necessary
- put a wavy line under any phrases which could be expressed in a shorter way.

b   Write out the reduced report, leaving out the excluded words and expressing the remaining information more concisely wherever possible.

c   Check your report for mistakes, then give it to your teacher.

Text 2D contains extracts from the diary of a Bosnian girl, Zlata Filipović, written during the civil war following the break-up of Yugoslavia. Here she describes her normal, happy life before the war reaches her home town of Sarajevo.

Text 2D

Monday, 2 December 1991

It's my birthday tomorrow. Mummy is making a cake and all the rest, because we really celebrate in our house. One day is for my friends, that's 3 December, and the next day is for family friends and relatives. Mummy and I are getting a tombola together, and thinking up questions for the children's quiz. This year we have birthday cups, plates and napkins all with little red apples on them. They're sweet. Mummy bought them in Pula. The cake will be shaped like a butterfly and . . . this time I'll be blowing out eleven candles. I'll have to take a deep breath and blow them all out at once.

Thursday, 19 December 1991

Sarajevo has launched an appeal (on TV) called 'Sarajevo Helps the Children of Dubrovnik'. In Srdjan's parcel we put a nice New Year's present for him to give to some child in Dubrovnik. We made up a package of sweets, chocolates, vitamins, a doll, some books, pencils, notebooks – whatever we could manage, hoping to bring happiness to some innocent child who has been stopped by the war from going to school, playing, eating what he wants and enjoying his childhood. It's a nice little package. I hope it makes whoever gets it happy. That's the idea. I also wrote a New Year's card saying I hoped the war in Dubrovnik would end soon.

8 Discuss as a class the style and content of Text 2D.

   a Which of the following types of content do you think Text 2D contains? Find an example for each of the types you select.

      narrative   description   opinion   fact   thought   feeling

   b How many tenses are used in the passage, and what is the effect of the range of tenses?

   c How can you tell that the passage was written by an 11-year-old?

9   **a**   Join the first sentence of Text 2D to the second sentence using a connective other than *and* or *so*.

      b   Include the information from the following three sentences from the passage in one complex sentence.

> This year we have birthday cups, plates and napkins all with little red apples on them. They're sweet. Mummy bought them in Pula.

      c   Make the following two sentences from the passage into one sentence, beginning 'I'll have to take a deep breath . . .'

> The cake will be shaped like a butterfly and . . . this time I'll be blowing out eleven candles. I'll have to take a deep breath and blow them all out at once.

      d   Replace the word *nice*, used twice in the second diary entry, with two more specific adjectives.

      e   Look at the use of *whoever* and *whatever* in the passage. What is the rule for the use of these words? Write a sentence including the word *whichever*.

10   **a**   Plan and write a single diary entry for the day before a big family event or festivity. You can use a real memory or make something up. Include the following:
- narrative, description, opinion, fact, thought, feeling
- a range of tenses
- complex sentences.

      b   Read your diary entry to the class.

Nadal seizes the crown for Spain

World No. 2 Rafael Nadal overcame Juan Martin del Potro of Argentina in an exciting thriller match at Seville's Olympic Stadium on Sunday, winning the fifth Davis Cup title for his country.

The classic contest lasted 4 hours 8 minutes. Nadal was completely dominated at the start of the match as del Potro raced out of the blocks and won seven straight games to take a set and a break lead, but the world No. 2 snatched a crucial game at the start of the second set that swung the momentum.

When Nadal broke service again to win the second set, it looked as though he was on his way to a comfortable victory. He walked through the third set and went a break up at the start of the fourth, but then del Potro, lifted by the Argentine fans, staged a remarkable comeback. In an enthralling fourth set, which swung one way and then the other on more than a few

occasions, del Potro served to take the match into a decider, only for Nadal to break back.

A few moments later the Spaniard found himself serving for the match, but this time it was del Potro who broke back. The match headed into a tiebreak and Nadal immediately took control, never looking back. He was utterly ruthless and completed the perfect 'golden' breaker with a winning forehand, a shot which sealed Spain's crown as Davis Cup champion for the fifth time.

www.khelopakistan.com

 Working with a partner, make notes on the report of a tennis match in Text 2E. Look at the following characteristics:

a   the type of vocabulary and imagery

b   the type of sentences, their length, and how they are constructed

c   the overall structure of the report, and how a match report differs from an ordinary news report.

 a   Think of a competitive game or a sports fixture, either real or imaginary, international or local (e.g. a chess tournament or a football match). It could be a school event.

b   Using your notes from Activity 11 to help you, make notes for a match report of your chosen event.

c   Write your report, of about one page divided into two columns. Use the tip on the next page to help you. Give it a headline and check it for accuracy before giving it to your teacher.

For Activity 12
Match reports

All matches have in common the element of competition and of there being a winner and a loser, so reports often stress the excitement of the contest and how evenly matched the opponents were in order to generate reader interest. The verbs are strong and may relate to battle imagery (e.g. *duel, dominate*). The adjectives and adverbs are also extreme or dramatic (e.g. *enthralling, desperate, utterly, overwhelmingly*).

Sentences tend to be long and complex, with several subordinate clauses, carefully ordered to build up to a climax or reversal. Clichés such as *more than a few, never looked back* and *remarkable comeback* are common.

Text 2F gives facts about playing cards in random order.

Playing cards

- complete set is called a pack or a deck; a few cards are called a hand
- can be used for building a house of cards, performing tricks, telling fortunes
- many types of card game for different numbers of players, including Patience for single player
- each of the 4 suits consists of 13 cards: the numerals 1–10 plus 3 court cards: King, Queen and Knave or Jack
- used for games of both skill and luck; nearly all games require similar cards to be collected
- back of cards have uniform design; front of cards depict the value of the card
- cards are shuffled to randomise their order in the pack
- by the 15th century, the four suits of spades, hearts, diamonds and clubs were in use
- invented in Ancient China in the Tang Dynasty
- a pack has four suits: two black (spades and clubs); two red (diamonds and hearts)
- entered Europe via Egypt in the 14th century
- in many card games the no. 1 card, called the Ace, is the highest value, although it is sometimes also a one
- reversible cards were designed so that they could be used easily both ways up
- the Joker card was a recent invention, in the USA; based on the court jester or fool figure; can usually take the place of any other card

- the pack is regarded as symbolic for the number of weeks in the year
- cards and card games have featured in many books and films
- card games, and the design of cards, vary between countries, but many features of the cards and of the games played with them are universal

13 Imagine that you are going to give a short talk to the class about playing cards.

a Read and then reread the facts in Text 2F. On a copy of the text, put numbers next to the facts to sequence them in a chronological and logical order. Make sure there is no repetition of facts.

b Copy out the facts as notes in the order you have decided on. Then group together, using brackets, those which are linked by topic, to show that these would be in the same sentence or paragraph in your talk.

c Compare your list of notes with a partner's. Discuss whose list is in the best order and contains the best groupings, and why.

14 Now you really are going to give a short talk to the class, of about three minutes, about a game or sport of your choice. First read the key point on the next page about giving a talk.

a Write down in note form what you already know about the subject. This may include examples and personal experience.

b Do some internet research to find more factual information and statistics to include, and make notes.

c Decide on the order in which you will use a combination of your two sources of information.

d On a small card, make headings of key words which show the talk topics and their sequence, to remind you what to say next. You may wish to consider using visual aids, such as photographs or equipment, to illustrate your talk.

e Rehearse your talk, checking the timing so that it is not too long or too short.

f Deliver your talk fluently and clearly. Think about your body language as well as your voice.

g Ask the class if they have any questions, and answer them.

h What mark out of ten would you give yourself for your talk, and why? Think about its structure, style and delivery. How did it compare with the talks of others in your class?

Key point

Giving a talk

- It is easier for an audience to follow a talk if there is a clear and connected sequence to the information it contains. If there are points which are in the wrong time order or which do not appear to be linked to each other, the audience may get confused.
- Details, examples and references to your personal experience make a talk more engaging and original.
- Visual aids can add to the effectiveness and enjoyment of a talk, but be careful not to let them become a distraction or play too important a role.
- Intonation and fluent delivery are necessary to keep your audience attentive; use variety of voice and a reasonable pace.
- The best way to ensure continuity is to have your ideas on a card as notes to be quickly glanced at so that you don't have to stop and try to remember what to say next.
- Make eye contact with your audience as much as possible – and even smile sometimes!
- If you sound enthusiastic about the content of your talk, then it is likely that your audience will be interested too.

UNIT 3 Water

In this unit you will read personal accounts of experiences, both factual and figurative, and you will write your own report. You will practise defining, organising, paraphrasing and explaining, as well as describing creatively. More grammar, punctuation and spelling points will be introduced.

Activities

1

a What does water mean to you? Quickly make notes of the words and associations which come into your head when you think of water. Contribute to a class brainstorm on the board.

b With a partner, list all the different types and purposes of water you can think of (e.g. rain, reservoir).

c With a partner, agree on and write a definition of water. Then compare your definition with dictionary versions.

2 **a** Can you think of any proverbs about water? Share them with the class.

b With a partner, work out what you think each saying means.
  i   The rain drenches everyone. (African)
  ii It never rains but it pours. (English)
  iii Heavy rain doesn't last long. (Italian)
  iv Into each life some rain must fall. (American)
  v   Roof can fool sun, but roof can't fool rain. (Caribbean)
  vi To the ant, a few drops of rain are a flood. (Japanese)
  vii The rain wets the leopard but it doesn't wash out its spots. (African)
  viii Don't empty the water jar until the rain falls. (Filipino)

c Feed back to the class some of your explanations and compare them with those of other pairs.

The sea

The sea is a hungry dog,
Giant and grey.
He rolls on the beach all day.
With his clashing teeth and shaggy jaws
Hour upon hour he gnaws
The rumbling, tumbling stones,
And 'Bones, bones, bones, bones!'
The giant sea-dog moans,
Licking his greasy paws.

And when the night wind roars
And the moon rocks in the stormy cloud,
He bounds to his feet and snuffs and sniffs,
Shaking his wet sides over the cliffs,
And howls and hollos long and loud.

But on quiet days in May or June,
When even the grasses on the dune
Play no more their reedy tune,
With his head between his paws
He lies on the sandy shores,
So quiet, so quiet, he scarcely snores.

James Reeves

3 a The poem in Text 3A is a sustained metaphor. Can you explain what this means? Do you think the device is successful?

b Look at the rhyme scheme of the poem. Also look at the use of repeated vocabulary and sound through alliteration, assonance and consonance. What is the effect of the repetition?

c Think of another sustained metaphor for the sea (e.g. 'The sea is a magnet'). Make notes to show the different ways in which your metaphor is an appropriate comparison, and share your idea with the class.

In Text 3B an adult describes going back to a place by the sea where he used to play as a child.

The bay

On the road to the bay was a lake of rushes
Where we bathed at times and changed in the bamboos.
Now it is rather to stand and say:
How many roads we take that lead to Nowhere,
The alley overgrown, no meaning now but loss:
Not that veritable garden where everything comes easy.

And by the bay itself were cliffs with carved names
And a hut on the shore beside the Maori ovens.
We raced boats from the banks of the **pumice** creek
Or swam in those autumnal shallows
Growing cold in amber water, riding the logs
Upstream, and waiting for the **taniwha**.

So now I remember the bay and the little spiders
On driftwood, so poisonous and quick.
The carved cliffs and the great outcrying surf
With currents round the rocks and the birds rising.
A thousand times an hour is torn across
And burned for the sake of going on living.
But I remember the bay that never was
And stand like stone and cannot turn away.

James K. Baxter

| pumice | a rough volcanic rock |
| taniwha | a sea monster in Maori mythology |

4 In small groups, analyse the message and language of the poem in Text 3B.

    a Discuss what point you think the poem is making, and the irony of the poem.

    b List the emotions the persona is feeling, and the quotations which show these feelings.

    c Pick out some phrases describing the water, and explain why they are effective.

    d What do you think the last four lines are saying? Express them in your own words.

    e Feed back your responses to the class in a discussion of the poem, which should also:
- compare the descriptions of the sea in Texts 3A and 3B
- compare the attitude of the persona to the sea in both poems
- say which poem you prefer, and why.

5 Working with a partner, you are going to describe the process shown in the diagram below.

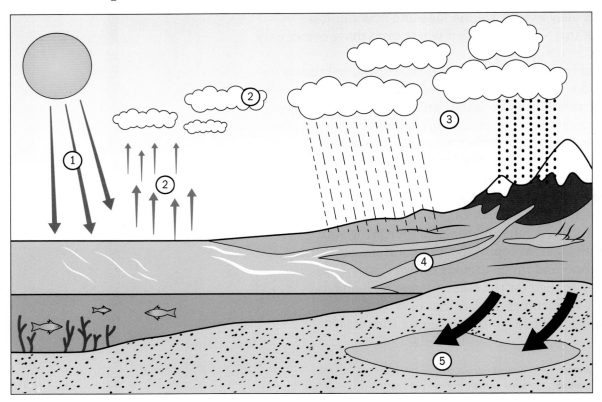

Diagram of the water cycle

a Study the diagram of the water cycle and discuss what is happening in it.

b Describe the process in writing, in five numbered stages. Use the tip below to help you.

c Read out your process description to the class, and notice whether those of other pairs are different.

For Activity 5b
Describing a process

Stages in a process are described clearly and concisely, using simple sentences, the present tense, and active verbs (e.g. 'Rain falls on high ground'). It is important that the stages are in a logical and chronological order. The vocabulary must be precise so that the information is accurate and the description matches the diagram.

Haiku

At the hidden pond
a fat frog plops like a stone
into the water

Magical water
transparent chameleon
colouring the world

 a Look at the two examples in Text 3C to help you define a haiku.
  i What kind of poem is a haiku?
  ii How many syllables does it contain and how are they divided between the lines?
  iii What can you say about the language of the poems?

b Think of a water feature to write a haiku about (e.g. a lake). Read the key point on the next page and then draft several versions. Ask your partner to help you choose the best one.

c Write out your haiku (or tanka – see the key point) and read it to the class; then illustrate it to be displayed.

Key point

Haiku

A haiku is a descriptive poem in the Japanese tradition which consists of three lines in a pattern of 5, 7, 5 syllables. The final line brings together the two images in lines one and two. Often there is a word to indicate which season the poem is set in.

The aim is to capture simply an intense moment in nature or to define a natural phenomenon figuratively using the power of description; a haiku should need no explanation as the actions or images speak for the feelings.

If you are feeling brave, you could go on to try to write a tanka, another Japanese poetic form, which has two more lines than a haiku, both of 7 syllables. This type of poetry is called syllabic verse; metre is irrelevant and rhyme is not required. You don't have to put in punctuation if it would spoil the flow of the poem. The devices used are personification, metaphors, similes, alliteration and assonance.

Text 3D

A drink of water

The time when the rains didn't come for three months and the sun was a yellow furnace in the sky was known as the Great Drought in Trinidad. It happened when everyone was expecting the sky to burst open with rain to fill the dry streams and water the parched earth.

But each day was the same, the sun rose early in a blue sky, and all day long the farmers lifted their eyes, wondering what had happened to Parjanya, the rain god. They rested on their hoes and forks and wrung perspiration from their clothes, seeing no hope in labour, terrified by the thought that if no rain fell soon they would lose their crops and livestock and face starvation and death.

In the tiny village of Las Lomas, somewhere in the field, a cow mooed mournfully, sniffing around for a bit of green in the cracked earth. The field was a desolation of drought. The trees were naked and barks peeled off trunks as if they were diseased. When the wind blew, it was heavy and unrelieving, as if the heat had taken all the spirit out of it.

Bush fires had swept Las Lomas and left the garden plots charred and smoking. Cattle were dropping dead in the heat. There was scarcely any water in the village; the river was dry with scummy mud.

But suddenly silence and darkness fell together. A large black blob of cloud blotted out the moon. The sky was thick with clouds piling up on each other and there was a new coolness in the wind. The sky grew black; it looked as if the moon had never been there. The wind became stronger; there was a swift fall of some heavy drops. Then the wind died like a sigh. A low rumble in the east – then silence. Perhaps Parjanya was having a joke with them; perhaps there would be no rain after all.

And then it came sweeping in from the north-east, with a rising wind. Not very heavy at first, but in thrusts, coming and going. The villagers opened their mouths and laughed, and water fell in. They shouted and cried and laughed again. Their cheeks were streaming, perhaps with tears, perhaps with Parjanya's rain.

Samuel Selvon

 7 **a** On a copy of Text 3D, circle the semi-colons (;). Decide what purpose they serve, and how a semi-colon differs from a full stop and a comma.

b When you have read the key point below, look back at the semi-colons you have circled in the passage. Decide whether to replace them with a full stop or with a comma and a connective.

c Now find two other places in the passage where semi-colons could have been used. Feed back to the class all your decisions for this activity.

Key point

Semi-colons

As you would expect, semi-colons are stronger than commas and less strong than full stops. They have the same function as full stops – to show where a sentence ends – but they do not require a capital letter after them. They suggest that there is a strong link in content between the two sentences they connect, and that therefore a full stop would be too definite.

Often the sentences joined by a semi-colon are balanced in their construction (see the last sentence in the penultimate paragraph of Text 3D), or at least one of the two sentences is short. A comma could not be used instead of a semi-colon, because a comma requires a connective and a semi-colon does not: for example, 'The river was dry; there had been no rain' or 'The river was dry, because there had been no rain.'

Semi-colons are not used as often as either full stops or commas, but try to include one in each of your pieces of writing, if appropriate, to show your ability to use a range of punctuation.

8 a The sentence structures, vocabulary and imagery are very simple in Text 3D. Look at the passage again to find some examples of each. Discuss with the class why you think this is.

b Underline on a copy of the passage any non-sentences you can find. Discuss with the class why you think they have been used. Use the tip below to help you.

c Contrast and parallels (repeated grammatical structures) have been used as devices in the passage. Find examples and discuss their effect.

For Activity 8b
Non-sentences

A non-sentence is one which does not contain a finite verb, i.e. a verb which shows subject and tense. They are generally to be avoided in continuous writing, but just occasionally you may come across one – or wish to use one – to draw attention to some aspect of the content of the writing. For example, the writer may wish to give the impression of speed, or suddenness, or to emphasise something just said, as in 'Nothing happened. Nothing at all.' (The first of these is a sentence; the second is not.) Non-sentences can often be found in dialogue, or at the very end of a piece of writing, for dramatic effect.

9 You are now going to write your own one-page account of a sudden change in the weather, using Text 3D as a model of structure and style.

a Decide on a setting and what the change in the weather will be.

b Draft two paragraphs describing the present situation, using descriptive language and imagery.

c Then write a paragraph to describe how the situation suddenly changes, using language which contrasts with the previous description.

d Think about where you could effectively use:
  • participle phrases with present or past participles
  • semi-colons
  • non-sentences and grammatical repetitions (but only a few).

e When you have finished editing and improving your draft, make a final copy, give it a title, and give it to your teacher.

Text 3E

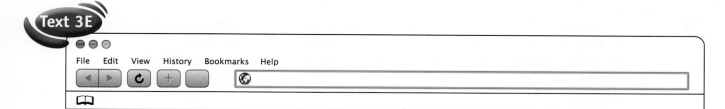

File   Edit   View   History   Bookmarks   Help

Toys spend 20 years at sea

Known as the Friendly Floatees, the Duck Armada, or the Moby Ducks, tiny yellow plastic bath ducks are still **circumnavigating** the globe 20 years after falling into the ocean in January 1992. *Loaded* as a shipment from China to North America, the container was swept overboard in the hurricane winds of the Pacific, and 30,000 bath toys set off on a journey on more **turbulent** waters than the bathtub they were intended for. The container actually included blue turtles, red beavers and green frogs, but it is the yellow ducks that have captured the imagination.

Thousands of the toys are still adrift, moving in flotillas, *trapped* in currents that stretch from Japan to California. They have been found in the area in which the Titanic sank. Scientists have been tracking the toys' movements to learn more about ocean currents, which affect the climate of the planet. Faded floatees have washed up all over the world, from Alaska to Australia, or been found trapped in ice; some are thought to have travelled up to 8000 kilometres. Originally the company which **manufactured** them offered a $100 reward for finding one; now they have become a collectors' item and can be bought on eBay for $2000.

Considered to be a **cute** story, it also has a serious side to it. Plastic which is ground up by the ocean then enters the food chain, *consumed* by birds and fish. There is an ever-growing level of plastic compared with plankton in the ocean. It is a poison and will appear on our dinner plates. There are estimates that there are 10,000 container spills a year, and many of these cargoes – e.g. computers, trainers, gloves – consist of **toxic** substances. And only 3% of the toys have been found so far.

10 **a** Find synonyms for the words in bold in Text 3E, giving the same part of speech. Try to work out the meaning of the words from their context before looking in a dictionary or thesaurus.

circumnavigating   turbulent   manufactured   cute   toxic

b The word *flotilla* is used in the passage as a collective noun for a group of floating things. Make a copy of the lists below. Work in small groups to see if you can work out which collective noun belongs to which aquatic creature, choosing from the words below to fill in the gaps. Guess the ones you don't know. Look at the tip on the next page to help you. You can compete with other groups to see who is first to complete the list correctly.

a bale   f congregation   c school   d pod   e shoal
f smack   g bloat   h bob   i knot   j bevy

   i   a _b_ of crocodiles   vi   a _bloat_ of jellyfish
   ii   a _d_ of whales   vii a _b_ of otters
   iii a _pod_ of dolphins   viii a _e_ of seals
   iv   a _c_ of fish   ix   a _j_ of toads
   v   a _a_ of hippopotami   x   a _a_ of turtles

c Look at the five words in italics in Text 3E.
   i   What part of speech are they?
   ii   How are they being used?

For Activity 10b
Collective nouns

There are many collective nouns in English, especially to describe a group of animals of the same kind. Mammals are usually in a herd or a pack, but birds and fish have a wider range of collective nouns, some of which are unexpected (e.g. a parcel of penguins). Often the word describes something about the animals' behaviour or movement.

Key point

Phrases with past participles

You have learnt how present participle phrases can be used instead of main (finite) verbs to make sentences more varied. You can also use past participles in this way, so that instead of starting a new sentence with 'They are trapped in currents', we can make expression more concise by joining this information to the sentence with a past participle and comma. As with present participle phrases, they can be positioned before or after the main clause, but the subject of both parts of the sentence must be the same.

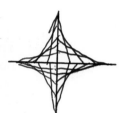

11 You are going to summarise, in one sentence for each paragraph, the key information in the web article in Text 3E.

a Using a copy of Text 3E, first delete all the information which you think is unnecessary because it is a detail, example, repetition or opinion.

b Then collect the remaining essential information in a plan, using your own words and making the expression more concise.

c Write out your three sentences, using present participles and past participles to help you form longer sentences. You can read your summary to the class and notice the differences compared with those of other students.

Text 3F

File   Edit   View   History   Bookmarks   Help

Walking sharks

In 2006 walking sharks were discovered in Indonesia. They are nocturnal sharks which have fins different from any other species, which allow them to walk across the sea bed. Their usual diet is shellfish. Indonesia contains some of the clearest water and richest reefs for biodiversity on the planet. The adults are about one metre long. Their bodies are sinuous, like lizards, and their faces can be seen as comical. The males and females mix together, unlike other sharks. When they are disturbed, they simply walk away, without attempting to swim.

Leatherback turtles

Leatherback turtles, which spend nearly all their lives at sea, are famous for making epic voyages across oceans. It has recently been discovered how good they are at navigation. The gigantic females – which can grow to two metres long – can swim for thousands of kilometres in a straight line. They journey from Central Africa to South America, following the shortest possible route across the Atlantic. It is not known exactly how they achieve this feat, but they may use the position of the sun and stars to guide them. Researchers attached satellite tracking devices to the shells of 25 females journeying from Gabon to Uruguay. It took them 150 days to complete the crossing. There are two other migration routes which they use.

12 Write two fact boxes, in note form, one for walking sharks and one for leatherback turtles. Each should contain ten items of information from the encyclopedia entries in Text 3F. The first fact in each box has been provided below.

Walking sharks	Leatherback turtles
discovered in 2006	famous for long sea journeys

Text 3G is adapted from a magazine article.

 Text 3G

THE LIFE OF A SRI LANKAN STILT FISHERMAN

I always wake when the sun rises. I get onto my stilt only on the days when the fish are running, and when the waves are not too high. Between December and April are the best months, before the monsoon comes. The fish don't see the silver hook in the white water. Sardines are the easiest to catch and they can be used as bait for bigger fish, but they earn less.

I always go to the same spot, which has always been the place used for many generations by my family. Stilts used to be made of wood but the sea causes damage and now we use metal. I push the six-metre-long stilt into the reef until it is deep enough to take my weight, which means about a third of it is underwater. There is a cross-step to support me while I fish, but nothing to hold me on. I use a rod and line – and a net for bringing in the bigger fish – and then I keep them in a bag attached to my body until I have finished.

I spend a couple of hours fishing in the morning, and a few hours more in the evening if it is worth returning. It's very relaxing, thinking of nothing except fish. I get paid about five rupees per fish, depending on the size, and sell them in the main town. The big fishing boats have large nets which catch many fish, and so we stilt fishermen end up with fewer fish and less money than in the old days. But on a good day I can still catch between 500 and 1000 fish. There's always luck involved.

I started fishing when I was a child. My children are not interested in continuing the family tradition, and in ten years' time I shall be too old and shall have to give up. This way of fishing may soon stop for ever, but I hope not.

Adapted from Sunday Times Magazine

13 **a** The following words are adjectives describing measurement. Give the irregular noun in each case. Check in a dictionary to see if you have the right spelling.

high	deep	wide	long	broad

hight depths widen length

b Give the past participle of each of these irregular verbs used in Text 3G.

wake	rise	get	come	catch
hold	keep	spend	sell	give

c Copy and complete this table of adjectives of amount used in Text 3G.

much	more	most
many	more	most
little	less	least
few	less	fewest

Key point

Countable and uncountable nouns

Whether we use *much* or *many*, *little* or *few*, *more* or *fewer* depends on whether the noun the adjective is qualifying is plural and can be counted or not. For example, we say 'much sugar' but 'many cups'; 'little faith' but 'few ideas'. Although money is composed of coins and notes, which can be counted, money itself is treated as an uncountable singular noun and we say, for example, 'He has too much money.' There are other common nouns in English used in the singular which are often plural in other languages, such as *information* and *news*, which are preceded by *much* rather than *many*.

It is a common mistake for people to use *less* where they should use *fewer* (e.g. they say 'less people'). *Little* is not to be confused with *a little*: 'There was little hope' stresses the absence of hope, whereas 'There was a little hope' is more positive. Likewise *few* and *a few* work in the same way.

Text 3H

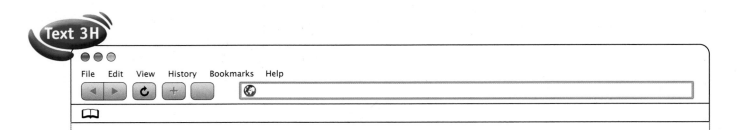

Water sports activities in New Zealand

Diving/snorkelling

Wellington's one-on-one diving specialists cater for small groups and backpackers. We can take you diving, snorkelling, or give you training any day of the week. There is a magical underwater world, with an unbelievable variety of exotic fish, just waiting for you to discover it.

Whitewater rafting   *no Jet*

Take up the offer of an amazing half-day whitewater rafting excursion out of Rotorua, including the Kaituna River and its 7-metre waterfall. This is the highest commercially rafted waterfall on earth, but there's nothing to fear: almost anyone can do it – no previous experience required.

Safari sightseeing   *Ad water Jet*

No New Zealand holiday is complete without a cruise. Haast River Safari on the west coast takes place in enclosed river boats, so you remain warm and dry while enjoying the great visibility and a freshly caught seafood meal. This is a unique, safe and comfortable experience suitable for all age groups.

Kayaking   *no Jet*

Kayaking in Queenstown is a great way to enjoy magnificent scenery while having fun in an eco-friendly way. We offer a variety of options to suit all levels of kayaker. Many of our excursions offer history and wildlife as well, with an expert commentary.

Jet boating   *Jet*

Just north of Queenstown, you can experience the most thrilling ride of your life as you twist and turn down the Shotover River and through Skippers Canyon at high speeds, manoeuvring your jet boat through sheer cliffs and overhanging walls while fishtailing, power braking and doing 360-degree spins. For the dare-devils amongst you, this is the ultimate sensational water sports experience.

Swim with dolphins   *water*

Just what you have always dreamed about: a day spent getting up close and personal with dolphins. Enjoy the beauty of the rolling rural landscape of North Canterbury as you travel by coach to the mountainous coast. Kaikoura has a world famous variety of marine mammals which includes not only the playful, people-friendly dolphins but also the grand spectacle of giant sperm whales.

Sailing   *no Jet*

Nothing can beat sailing around the beautiful Bay of Islands – all 144 of them – on-board a 25-metre maxi-yacht. You can be a member of the crew and get involved by helping with ropes and sails, and even taking a turn at the helm. Or you can just sit back, relax, watch and enjoy the sailing adventure.

14 a What are the different categories of water sports on offer in Text 3H? How would you group them? Write headings in your notebook.

b What are the features that the different sports have in common? Write a sentence, in your own words, of what is attractive about New Zealand water sports.

c Imagine that you and a friend are allowed to do one of the sports listed in Text 3H as a birthday treat. Write a dialogue in your notebook, speaking five times each, starting with yourself, in which you and your friend arrive at a decision about which one to choose, after evaluating and arguing about the options. You can perform your dialogues to the class.

15 Imagine that during your water sports activity you saw something very strange in the water. You are going to write an eyewitness account of your sighting, using the tip below to help you.

a Discuss in class what kind of water monsters are reported and in what circumstances. You can research on the internet to give you ideas (e.g. www.mysterycasebook.com/lakemonsterphotographs.html).

b Decide on your 'monster'. Make notes of where and when you saw it, who you were with, what you were doing, what it was doing, and what finally happened.

c Put your notes into the right order to give a chronological account of the incident.

d Draft your report, thinking about suitable expression and tone for someone in authority whom you do not know.

e Make a final copy of your report, check it and give it to your teacher.

For Activity 15
Formal reports

A witness statement is a kind of formal report and it is essential that it should be detailed and accurate as it is an official document. All the necessary and relevant information should be included to make it sound convincing. State at the beginning who you are, where you are from and how you came to be in that place at that time. Include the exact details of date, time, place and weather conditions. The style should be objective and impersonal; the report should stick to the facts without using figurative language or giving opinions.

UNIT 4 The feast

Descriptive writing devices are the focus of this unit. You will also practise reading and writing blank verse and dramatic dialogue, and think about how character and humour are created. The activities include looking at adjectival endings and time adverbs, and more vocabulary building.

Activities

1 **a** Think of all the associations the word *feast* has for you (e.g. a celebration). See how many you can contribute to a list on the board.

b Think of all the times in the year in your country when people gather together for a special meal. Contribute to a list on the board.

c The idea of feasting is linked to the idea of fasting. Write a sentence to explain the connection.

Text 4A is an extract from a famous poem in which a feast is set out.

Text 4A

> While he from forth the closet brought a heap
> Of candied apple, quince, and plum, and gourd;
> With jellies soother than the creamy curd,
> And lucent syrops, tinct with cinnamon;
> Manna and dates, in argosy transferr'd
> From Fez; and spiced dainties, every one,
> From silken Samarcand to cedar'd Lebanon.
>
> These delicates he heap'd with glowing hand
> On golden dishes and in baskets bright
> Of wreathed silver: sumptuous they stand
> In the retired quiet of the night,
> Filling the chilly room with perfume light.
>
> *From 'The Eve of St Agnes' by John Keats*

| manna | miraculous heavenly food |
| argosy | fleet of merchant ships |

2 In this activity you will study closely the vocabulary of Text 4A.

a Look at the following ten adjectives from Text 4A. Look up the meaning of any you don't know. Comment in a class discussion on their sound and meaning, what they make you think of, and their effect on the description.

i candied	iv silken	vii golden	ix sumptuous
ii soother	v cedar'd	viii wreathed	x perfume
iii lucent	vi glowing		

b Select nouns from the extract which you think have a powerful effect, and explain why their effect is powerful.

c Discuss the effect of the use of place names in the extract.

3 With a partner, you are going to write a comic playscript based on a picnic scene. First read the key point on the next page.

a Decide what the contents of your perfect picnic basket would be.

b Create two characters and a setting for a picnic scene. Then write a page of dialogue for the characters, which includes references to the food. Try to make the dialogue humorous in some way. You can add stage directions (see the key point on the next page and the tip on page 50) to show how gesture and movement convey character.

c Perform your dialogue to the rest of the class. (It would be better if you could learn it and perform it without needing to look at the script.) Comment on each other's dialogues and performances.

Key point

Comic writing

There are various standard devices used in comic writing:

- Exaggeration is one, and here it could be the quantity of food in the picnic basket.
- Mismatching of characters causes them to misunderstand or disapprove of each other.
- If the characters are out of place in their setting, or unable to cope with the situation they are in, this creates humour.
- You can also use the unexpected, such as when the characters' roles are suddenly reversed (e.g. the brave one suddenly becomes timid).
- Bizarre behaviour or appearance can have a humorous effect, and this can be suggested through stage directions; there is a famous one in a Shakespeare play: 'Exit, pursued by a bear'.

For Activity 3b
Stage directions

Stage directions give actors information about the movements, gestures and tone of voice to use, which might not be clear from the wording of the script, though as much as possible should be indicated by the words themselves. (Shakespeare used only the most basic and necessary of stage directions, such as 'They fight'.) For instance, if a speech is to be delivered in a sad or sarcastic voice, this should be recognisable from the kind of language being used. Typical stage directions say things like 'looking back over his shoulder' and 'trying to suppress a smile', or refer to the handling of props, as in 'picking up the basket', 'handing her the letter'. The conventional way to indicate stage directions, so that they are not confused with the dialogue, is to put them in square brackets or, if typewritten, in italics or capitals.

Text 4B is the story of the visit of a beggar to the house of a member of a noble Persian family of Baghdad.

Text 4B

Fake feast 1

There now remains for me to relate to you the story of my sixth brother, whose name was Schacabac. Like the rest of us, he inherited a hundred silver drachmas from our father, which he thought was a large fortune, but through ill-luck, he soon lost it all, and was driven to beg. As he had a smooth tongue and good manners, he really did very well in his new profession, and he devoted himself specially to making friends with the servants in big houses, so as to gain access to their masters.

One day he was passing a splendid mansion, with a crowd of servants lounging in the courtyard. He thought that from the appearance of the house it might yield him a rich harvest, so he entered and enquired to whom it belonged.

'My good man, where do you come from?' replied the servant. 'Can't you see for yourself that it can belong only to someone famed for their liberality and generosity?' My brother, hearing this, asked the porters, of whom there were several, if they would give him alms. They did not refuse, but told him politely to go in, and speak to the master himself.

My brother thanked them for their courtesy and entered the building, which was so large that it took him some time to reach the apartments of the master. At last, in a room richly decorated with paintings, he saw an old man with a long white beard, sitting on a sofa, who received him with such kindness that my brother was emboldened to make his petition.

'My lord,' he said, 'you <u>behold</u> in me a poor man who only lives by the help of persons as rich and as generous as you.'

Before he could proceed further, he was stopped by the astonishment shown by the master. 'Is it possible,' he cried, 'that while I am in Baghdad, a man like you should be starving? That is a state of things that must at once be put an end to! Never shall it be said that I have abandoned you, and I am sure that you, on your part, will never abandon me.'

'My lord,' answered my brother, 'I <u>swear</u> that I have not broken my fast this whole day.'

'What, you are dying of hunger?' exclaimed the master. 'Here, slave; bring water, that we may wash our hands before meat!' No slave appeared, but my brother remarked that the master did not fail to rub his hands as if the water had been poured over them.

Then he said to my brother, 'Why don't you wash your hands too?' and Schacabac, supposing that it was a joke on the part of the master (though he could see none himself), drew near, and imitated his motion.

When the master had done rubbing his hands, he raised his voice, and cried, 'Set food before us at once, we are very hungry.' No food was brought, but the master pretended to help himself from a dish, and carry a morsel to his mouth, saying as he did so, 'Eat, my friend, eat, I entreat. Help yourself as freely as if you were at home! For a starving man, you <u>seem</u> to have a very small appetite.'

'Excuse me, my lord,' replied Schacabac, imitating his gestures as before, 'I really am not losing time, and I do full justice to the repast.'

'How do you <u>like</u> this bread?' asked the master. 'I <u>find</u> it particularly good myself.'

'Oh, my lord,' answered my brother, who beheld neither meat nor bread, 'never have I tasted anything so delicious!'

After ordering a variety of dishes (which never came) to be placed on the table, and discussing the merits of each one, the master began to laugh, and embraced him heartily. 'I have long been seeking,' he exclaimed, 'a man of your description, and henceforth my house shall be yours. You have had the good grace to fall in with my humour, and to pretend to eat when nothing was there. Now you shall be rewarded by a really good supper.'

Then he clapped his hands, and all the dishes were brought that they had tasted in imagination before and during the repast, as slaves sang and played on various instruments. All the while Schacabac was treated by the master as a familiar friend, and dressed in a garment out of his own wardrobe.

From Tales from the Arabian Nights

a Pick out the 14 different time adverbs and adverbial phrases in Text 4B, i.e. the single words and short phrases which refer to when an event happened.

b What other time adverbs and adverbial phrases can you think of? List as many as you can.

c Write a summary of the events in Text 4B, in one paragraph, using a range of time adverbs and adverbial phrases. Read the key point on the next page to help you.

Key point

Time adverbs and adverbial phrases

In narrative, and in description of a process, a range of time adverbs and adverbial phrases needs to be used in order to give variety to the structuring of a chronological account. Some are quite vague (e.g. *later, afterwards, one day*) and others are very specific (e.g. *immediately, simultaneously, at midnight*). These give the writing sequence, linkage and pace. It is a common fault in writing to use *then* repetitively.

5 a There are some old-fashioned words in Text 4B. Find the words in the passage that mean the following:

i	tell	iv	given courage	vii	bit
ii	money	v	request	viii	meal
iii	politeness	vi	look at		

ix from now on
x   item of
    clothing

b Explain the following metaphors from the passage:
   • he had a smooth tongue
   • yield him a rich harvest
   • do full justice to.

c Look at the underlined verbs in the passage. How are they similar? What tense is being used? Now read the key point below.

Key point

Verbs of perception

Verbs of perception, which include beliefs and feelings, are used in the present simple (or past simple) tense even when they are describing something which is happening now and lasts for some time. For example, we say 'I feel sorry for that woman over there'; 'he saw the bus approaching from some way off', not 'I am feeling' or 'he was seeing'. There are many verbs in this category, including those to do with the five senses and with attitudes (e.g. *hear, know, approve*), so you must remember when you are writing not to use such verbs in the present continuous or past continuous.

In this scene from Shakespeare's play *The Tempest*, Prospero, the ex-Duke of Milan and now a magician, has caused a ship passing his Mediterranean island to sink so that he can get revenge, with the help of the spirit Ariel, on his brother Antonio. Twelve years previously, Antonio stole Prospero's title and sent him into exile with the help of Alonso, the King of Naples. The other characters are courtiers.

Fake feast 2

Solemn and strange music; enter PROSPERO *above, invisible*

ALONSO   What harmony is this? my good friends, hark!

GONZALO   Marvellous sweet music.

Enter several strange shapes, bringing in a banquet, and dance about it with gentle actions of salutations, and inviting the king, etc. to eat, they depart

ALONSO   Give us kind keepers, heavens! What were these?

SEBASTIAN   A living drollery! Now I will believe
That there are unicorns; that in Arabia
There is one tree, the phoenix' throne, one phoenix
At this hour reigning there.

ANTONIO   I'll believe both;
And what does else want credit, come to me
And I'll be sworn 'tis true. Travellers ne'er did lie,
Though fools at home condemn 'em.

GONZALO   If in Naples
I should report this now, would they believe me?
If I should say I saw such islanders –
For certes, these are people of the island –
Who though they are of monstrous shape, yet note
Their manners are more gentle, kind, than of
Our human generation you shall find
Many, nay almost any.

PROSPERO [*Aside*]   Honest lord,
Thou hast said well – for some of you there present
Are worse than devils.

ALONSO   I cannot too much muse,
Such shapes, such gesture, and such sound, expressing –
Although they want the use of tongue – a kind
Of excellent dumb discourse.

PROSPERO [*Aside*]   Praise in departing.

FRANCISCO   They vanished strangely.

SEBASTIAN   No matter, since they
Have left their viands behind; for we have stomachs.
Wilt please you taste of what is here?

ALONSO   Not I.
GONZALO   Faith, sir, you need not fear. When we were boys,
                 Who would believe that there were mountaineers,
                 Dewlapped like bulls, whose throats had hanging at 'em
                 Wallets of flesh? Or that there were such men
                 Whose heads stood in their breasts? Which now we find
                 Each putter-out of five for one will bring us
                 Good warrant of.
ALONSO   I will stand to, and feed,
                 Although my last, no matter, since I feel
                 The best is past. Brother, my lord the duke,
                 Stand to and do as we.

Thunder and lightning. Enter ARIEL, *like a* **harpy**, *claps his wings upon the table,*
and with a quaint device the banquet vanishes
ARIEL   You are three men of sin, whom Destiny –
                 That hath to instrument this lower world,
                 And what is in't – the never-surfeited sea
                 Hath caused to belch up you. And on this island,
                 Where man doth not inhabit – you 'mongst men
                 Being most unfit to live – I have made you mad;
                 And even with suchlike valour men hang and drown
                 Their proper selves.

> [*Alonso, Sebastian, Antonio draw their swords*]
>   You fools! I and my fellows
> Are ministers of Fate. The elements
> Of whom your swords are **tempered** may as well
> Wound the loud winds, or with bemocked-at stabs
> Kill the still-closing waters, as **diminish**
> **One dowl that's in my plume**. My fellow ministers
> Are like invulnerable. If you could hurt,
> Your swords are now too massy for your strengths,
> And will not be uplifted. But remember –
> For that's my business to you – that you three
> From Milan did supplant good Prospero;
> Exposed unto the sea – which **hath requit it** –
> Him, and his innocent child; for which foul deed,
> The powers, delaying, not forgetting, have
> Incensed the seas and shores, yea, all the creatures
> Against your peace. Thee of thy son, Alonso,
> They have bereft; and do pronounce by me
> **Ling'ring perdition** – worse than any death
> Can be at once – shall step by step attend
> You, and your ways; whose wraths to guard you from –
> Which here, in this most desolate isle, else falls
> Upon your heads – is nothing but heart's sorrow,
> And a clear life ensuing.

He vanishes in thunder

dewlapped	loose folds of skin hanging from beneath the chin
each putter-out of five for one	one in five travellers
harpy	a monster with a woman's head and a bird's body
tempered	made by mixing and heating metals
diminish one dowl that's in my plume	hurt one hair on my head
hath requit it	has taken revenge
ling'ring perdition	slow punishment

6 Read Text 4C to yourself, and underline words you do not know. Try to work out their meaning, before checking with your teacher, by thinking about:

- what other words they remind you of or contain within them
- their similarity to words in another language that you know
- what they are likely to mean in the context of the surrounding words and the situation the characters are in.

7 **a** Write a one-sentence summary of what is happening in this scene of the play (Text 4C).

b What do you think the point of the banquet is, which mysteriously appears and then disappears again?

c Judging from the extract in Text 4C, how would you describe the following characters? Write lists of adjectives which would describe their comments, attitudes and actions.
i   Alonso   iv Sebastian
ii Gonzalo   v Ariel
iii Antonio

8 Read Text 4C out loud around the class, one line each.

a What do you notice about the lines? Look at their length and metre.

b The play is written in blank verse. Decide with a partner what the definition of blank verse is.

c Read the key point, then write two lines, about anything at all, which are in blank verse. Read your lines to the class to see if they agree that they are in blank verse.

Key point

Blank verse

Modern plays are usually written in prose, and there is therefore no fixed length of line or rhyme scheme or metrical pattern. Shakespeare wrote his plays in blank verse, and so have many other playwrights and poets over many centuries. The definition is that it consists of unrhymed (blank) iambic pentameter, i.e. ten beats which alternate between unstressed and stressed syllables, e.g.

Who **would** be**lieve** that **there** were **mount**ain**eers**

Although some of the lines in Text 4C look shorter, they can be joined with the preceding half-line to make a whole line of blank verse. The lines are sometimes run on, or contain an extra syllable or an irregular stress, in order to avoid monotony and make the verse sound more like genuine speech. Occasionally they are rhymed, for special effect, and then they are called heroic couplets (because epic poems about heroes were written in this form).

Text 4D on the next page is from a travel guide section on the food to be found in a region of southern India.

Text 4D

Eating out in Puducherry

A place <u>which the locals rave about</u> is 'Satsanga', run by a Frenchman who left Paris 15 years ago. Here, locals <u>come in droves</u> to sit at the small tables in the outdoor courtyard and feast upon the **eclectic fusion** of French ingredients and Indian spices.

Over at the charming Hotel de l'Orient, you can sup <u>to your heart's content</u> on prawns in saffron sauce or, for the sweet-toothed, the coconut flan with caramel that is as close to perfection as one can get.

On every street corner there is a food shack or *dhaba* waiting to be discovered. Despite their generally **shabby** appearance, these small places serve some of the most **authentic** and delicious food around. *Dosa* meals are prepared <u>from scratch</u> in front of hungry customers, as are Mysore *bondas* (spicy deep-fried potato cakes).

Sweets and savouries <u>go hand in hand</u> in South India and are served on special occasions and as teatime treats for guests. Shops which sell sweet and savoury snacks are busy all year round, but the crowds really descend on them during the Hindu festivals of Diwali in October and Pongal in January, for which the festival dish consists of rice cooked with *jaggery* (unrefined sugar cane), raisins and nuts.

Visitors to Puducherry's **frenetic** Nellithope indoor fish market are greeted by the **heady** scent of red snappers, sardines, eels, spider crabs, mackerel and large prawns, all freshly hauled from the Bay of Bengal. It is here that you will find South India's most prized and **versatile** fish, the seer fish, which has a texture similar to tuna.

Another favourite in local households is a South Indian meat stew consisting of goat, seasoned with bay leaves, cinnamon,

star anise and fennel seeds, freshly grated coconut and a local vegetable known as drumstick (which tastes like marrow). The stew is served on a large banana leaf as part of the **delectable** *thali* (set meal) which also includes boiled cassava, spiced boiled eggs seasoned with chilli powder, fried fish, and lentil dishes of *sambar* and *rasam*. A Tamil meal should traditionally include six taste sensations: sweet, sour, salty, bitter, **pungent** and **astringent**.

Manju Malhi

9 Working with a partner, focus on the language of Text 4D.

a Give synonyms for the ten words in bold in the passage. Use a
thesaurus and choose the synonym which best fits the context.

i	eclectic	vi	heady
ii	fusion	vii	versatile
iii	shabby	viii	delectable
iv	authentic	ix	pungent
v	frenetic	x	astringent

b Paraphrase the following five expressions, which are underlined in
the passage.
   i   which the locals rave about
   ii come in droves
   iii to your heart's content
   iv from scratch
   v   go hand in hand

c Look at the adjectives in the passage and collect a list of the
different adjectival endings. Then complete the list with all the
other adjectival endings you can think of. Look at the key point
below if you need help.

Key point

Adjectival endings

Adjectives are often formed from the verb form (e.g. *attract → attractive*);
sometimes the consonant of the verb changes (e.g. *save → safe*). The
present participle or past participle verb form, ending in *ing* or *ed*, may
be used as an adjective (e.g. *charming, dazzling; fried, prized*). A common
adjectival ending, added to the noun, is *ful* (e.g. *colourful, hopeful*); the
opposite (negative) meaning is created by adding the suffix *less* (e.g.
colourless, hopeless). There are another dozen adjectival endings – some
of which are very similar, like *ant* and *ent*, *ible* and *able* – which have to
be learnt.

10 Your task is to write a description of this photograph, using the ideas you have learnt in this unit for how to make description lively and engaging.

a Collect exotic and unusual vocabulary, especially adjectives, and specific colour words which come to mind when you study the photograph.

b Decide on a framework for your description, entitled 'The feast': for example, describing items clockwise around the table; or approaching it from a distance and presenting what you see in order of size; or describing dishes in colour categories, or by type of food (e.g. fruit first).

c Draft your description, which should be about a page in length. Read it to the rest of the class.

Text 4E comes from a blog about food and cooking. American spelling and vocabulary are used.

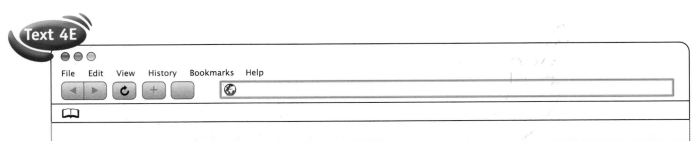

Text 4E

File   Edit   View   History   Bookmarks   Help

A visit to a souk

One of my favorite things to do is walk around the souks. I love losing myself in the crowds, talking with vendors, and taking in my surroundings. It's an exhilarating feeling. I have a hard time describing it, but the city brings me to life. The chatter, the people, the sales, the merchandise – it's all a very raw experience. There are souks for almost everything here: clothing, gold, jewelry, food – this is how traditional markets operate. The market I most often visit is a vegetable souk that's a convenient ten-minute walk from my house.

The first time I visited, I couldn't help but think this is what a real farmers' market must be like. Mountains of vegetables that look as though they have just been picked, and amazing prices. The *kibab* – small torpedo-shape balls, pointy on both ends, made from minced meat and fine *bulgur* (cracked wheat) – is a classic preparation across the Levant, and is famous for its endless variations: with sour cherries or quince; carrots or pumpkin; yogurt or broth; raw or cooked; fried or baked; boiled or grilled.

Souks are also known for their variety of stuffed vegetables: eggplants, zucchini, peppers, grape leaves, cabbage leaves, tomatoes, potatoes; I'm sure I'm forgetting a lot. As of lately, my favorite has been the stuffed Swiss chard leaves. I had them for the first time a few months ago on a chilly winter afternoon. My grandmother's sister prepared a batch one afternoon for me to try. The stuffed chard leaves looked almost like over-stuffed grape leaves, but with a more pronounced dark green color.

Before we sat down to eat, my grandmother's sister asked me to mince some garlic; it's for the sauce, she said. She added the fragrant garlic bits into a bowl of pearly white yogurt, sprinkled a small handful of dried mint, and stirred. It looked beautiful. The specks of bright green mint stood out in the creamy yogurt. As she carried the pot of stuffed chard leaves to the table she told me this used to be my grandfather's favorite dish. I took my first bite. I remember I wasn't very excited. In my mind, it didn't seem like anything could compare to the flavor and texture of stuffed grape leaves. 'You have to eat it with the yogurt sauce,' she proclaimed.

I took another bite, this time with the yogurt. Had I been a cartoon character, this is when fireworks would be happening in my eyes. The difference is incredible. The sauce brings the dish to life. The garlic flavor is intense, but the yogurt helps round out its sharp edges – it also helps cool the palate.

I practiced making this dish on my own, and I think I finally got it right. I got excellent reviews from a couple of expert home cooks. This is one of those dishes that takes time, but is worth every minute of rolling.

Tony Tahhan

Levant	Arabic region of the Eastern Mediterranean

11 Work with a partner to analyse the structure and language of Text 4E.

a What is the structure of the passage? Make notes on what you would call the different stages.

b What are the different elements of the passage and how do they contribute to its interest for the reader?

c Without looking back at the passage, write down which words from it you remember, and try to explain why. Give your feedback to the rest of the class.

12 Now discuss Text 4E as a class.

a What kind of sentences are mainly used in the passage? Why do you think this is, and what effect is created?

b Look again at the first three paragraphs of the passage. What grammatical and stylistic device do you notice?

c Why do you think this device is used in descriptive writing? Think about how it can be made interesting and varied. Read the tip below to help you.

For Activity 12c
Using lists in description

Generally, listing is not recommended in writing as it is a device which can be predictable, simplistic and unengaging. However, descriptive writing needs to include as much information as possible to create a picture for the reader, and listing can be an economical method of doing this, as shown in the first three paragraphs of Text 4E. Lists should be used sparingly though, and it is better if they are not always the same type of list. The aim in descriptive writing is to use variety of expression, in grammar and vocabulary, in order to avoid sounding factual and monotonous. Lists can take many forms, such as triplets of verbs, nouns, adjectives or phrases; similar or contrasting pairs (as at the end of paragraph two); words beginning with the same letter; opposite ends of a range, i.e. 'from . . . to . . .'

13 Imagine you are walking through a street market near your home. Write a page of an article for a magazine called 'A feast for the senses'. Look back at Texts 4D and 4E to give you ideas for content, structure and style. The tip below may also help you.

a Decide what the market is selling; it could be fruit and vegetables, or spices, or any other fresh local produce.

b Plan the structure for your writing.

c Write down some vocabulary, images and sense descriptions to use.

d Draft your description.

e Edit it to improve its range of expression and accuracy, then give it to your teacher.

For Activity 13
Descriptive devices

- In your magazine article you could use a structural framework of approaching the market and passing through it, or of visiting it at opening or closing time and describing the process of the change as things are opened up and displayed or packed away at the end. You could experiment with viewpoint, and describe the market first from a hill above it and then close up at ground level.

- This is a topic which lends itself to the use of description relating to all five senses, so make sure you have some of each to create the complete atmosphere.

- You may want to include lists; if so, think of ways of making them varied and interesting.

- Avoid repeating vocabulary and use unusual and precise words.

- Make sure that you have used enough details; usually each noun is qualified, i.e. described, by at least one adjective in descriptive writing.

- Remember that compound adjectives (e.g. *lily-white*, *silver-topped*) make your descriptions richer, more evocative and more precise.

UNIT **5** Other lives

This unit focuses on biographical writing, on adopting a different viewpoint and register, and on precise description. There are opportunities to write a formal letter, a job advertisement and a CV, as well as descriptive pieces. You will also practise new ways of forming sentences.

Activities

 a If you were not who you are, where would you like to be living and when?

b Write down the names of three historical figures who changed the world. Tell the class who they are, explaining why you chose them.

c Think of the living person you most admire and why. Contribute your ideas to a class discussion and see how many of your fellow students have made the same choice.

Nelson Mandela became the first black president of South Africa after spending 27 years in prison. The following extract from his autobiography, *Long Walk to Freedom,* is set in 1961 and describes his life under apartheid (racial segregation) and as a member of a banned organisation, the African National Congress.

Living underground

Living underground requires a **seismic psychological** shift. One has to plan every action, however small and seemingly **insignificant**. Nothing is innocent. Everything is questioned. You cannot be yourself, you must fully inhabit whatever role you have **assumed**.

I became a creature of the night. I would keep to my hideout during the day, and emerge to do my work when it became dark. I **operated** mainly from Johannesburg, but I would travel as necessary. I stayed in empty flats, in people's houses, wherever I could be alone and **inconspicuous**. Although I am a **gregarious** person, I love **solitude** even more. I welcomed the opportunity to be by myself, to plan, to think, to plot. But one can have too much solitude.

I was terribly lonesome for my wife and family.

The key to being underground is to be invisible. As a leader, one often seeks **prominence**; as an **outlaw**, the opposite is true. When underground I did not walk as tall or stand as straight. I spoke more softly, with less clarity and **distinction**. I was more passive, more **unobtrusive**; I did not ask for things but let people tell me what to do. I did not shave or cut my hair. My most frequent disguise was as a chauffeur, chef or a 'garden boy'. I would wear the blue overalls of the field-worker and often wore round, rimless glasses known as Mazzawatee tea-glasses. I had a car and I wore a chauffeur's cap with my overalls. The pose of chauffeur was convenient because I could travel under the **pretext** of driving my master's car.

During those early months, when there was a warrant for my arrest and I was being pursued by the police, my outlaw existence caught the imagination of the press. Articles claiming that I had been here and there were on the front pages. Roadblocks were **instituted** all over the country, but the police repeatedly came up empty-handed.

I travelled secretly about the country: I was with Muslims in the Cape, with sugar-workers in Natal, with factory workers in Port Elizabeth. I moved through townships in different parts of the country, attending secret meetings at night. I would pop up here and there to the annoyance of the police and to the delight of the people. There were many wild and inaccurate stories about my experiences underground. People love to **embellish** tales of daring. I did have a number of narrow escapes, however, which no one knew about.

2 Describe in one sentence each, according to Text 5A:

a Nelson Mandela's attitude to life while he was 'underground'

b the character of Nelson Mandela

c the kind of activities that he was engaged in.

3 **a** Give the meanings, in context, of each of the 15 words in bold in Text 5A. Guess any you do not know before checking in a dictionary.

b The first paragraph uses the idea of being 'underground' figuratively. Can you find the other words which continue the same metaphor in paragraph two?

c On a copy of Text 5A, circle the semi-colons. Then insert connectives (or present or past participles) to replace them. How do you think this changes the style of the writing? The tip on the next page will give you some ideas.

Tip

For Activity 3c
Connectives versus semi-colons

Sometimes a writer deliberately avoids using connectives, preferring either short, simple, separate sentences or those connected by just a semi-colon. If the subject matter is serious or painful – as in this account about being in constant danger – then a minimalist expression and flat tone, with no extra words and no fluency, can be appropriate. Long, complex, fluent sentence structures often give the opposite impression, one of vitality and well-being.

Text 5B

The life of Nobel Peace Prize Laureate Aung San Suu Kyi

Born in Burma (also known as Myanmar) in 1945, Aung San Suu Kyi was the only daughter of Aung San, considered to be the father of modern-day Burma. She attended high school in New Delhi and then studied philosophy, politics and economics at Oxford University. She moved to New York for graduate studies, where she worked as a hospital **volunteer**, helping patients learn to read. Following her marriage to Briton Michael Aris, she went to the Himalayan kingdom of Bhutan and worked in the Royal Ministry of Foreign Affairs, also writing several books about her country. Her two sons, born in the UK in 1973 and 1977, were initiated into monkhood in a traditional Buddhist ceremony.

The **suppression** by the military rulers of a mass uprising in Burma made Suu Kyi write a protest letter calling for democratic government of the country. In 1988 she formed a league to carry out non-violent civil disobedience and toured the country making speeches. She vowed to serve her country, even at the risk of death, as her father and mother had done, and continued her **campaign** despite the threats, arrests and killings of her followers. She was placed under house arrest with her sons in 1989, without charge or trial, and went on hunger strike on behalf of students arrested with her. Despite her detention, her National League for Democracy party won 82% of **parliamentary** seats in the election in 1990, but the rulers did not recognise the result.

After receiving various human rights prizes, she was awarded the Nobel Peace Prize in 1991 but was unable to collect it in Oslo as she was still detained, and refused to buy her freedom at the expense of withdrawing from politics. She announced that she would use the prize money to provide health and education facilities for the Burmese people. Her popularity continued to grow, at home and abroad. Suu Kyi discouraged tourists from visiting Burma and **businesses** from investing in the country until it was free. Her husband died in 1999; he had not seen her since 1995 and was refused permission to visit her one last time. She knew that if she left the country she would not be allowed to return.

Now, after spending 15 years of the past 21 under house arrest, Suu Kyi is at liberty. She has recently been elected to the Burmese parliament and travelled to Europe, where in June 2012 she finally made her acceptance speech for the Nobel Peace Prize, two decades late. She believes that she survived her ordeal because of the BBC world radio service – which allowed her to stay informed and feel in touch with the rest of the world and the lives of other people – and through playing the piano. She says, 'When I was under house arrest I thought that what I wanted to be most of all was a composer, because I thought then I could compose music and this could reach out to people all over the world, regardless of what language they knew or didn't know.' She believes that resolving conflict is not about condemnation but about discovering and solving the roots of the conflict.

4

a Explain orally what you have learnt about the character of Aung San Suu Kyi.

b i Write one-sentence definitions for the five words in bold in Text 5B, as they are used in the passage.

ii Study and practise the spelling of these five difficult words.

c **What do the following prefixes and suffixes mean, judging from these words from the passage?**

philo- (philosophy)   -hood (monkhood)   sub/p- (suppression)

sur- (survive)   con/m- (conflict, composer)

5 Working with a partner, imagine a journalist is sent to interview Aung San Suu Kyi.

a **Plan five questions for the journalist to ask her which relate to the information given in Text 5B.**

b **Script the interview between the journalist and the politician.**

c **i Read out your interviews to the class.**
  ii Give feedback on the interviews of other pairs.

Text 5C is an extract from *Chinese Cinderella*, the autobiography of Adeline Yen Mah, who was rejected by her stepmother.

After school was let out in the early afternoon, I waited with all the other first-graders by the school gate. One by one they were greeted and led away by their anxiously hovering mothers. Eventually, I was the only one left. Nobody had come for me. The metal gate slowly **clanged** shut behind me as I watched my classmates disperse, each clutching her mother's hand and eagerly recounting the adventures of her first day at school. After a long time, I peered through a crack into the deserted playground. Not a person was in sight. Cautiously, I pushed against the massive iron gate. It was firmly locked. Trembling with fear, I realised that nobody was coming to pick me up. Too embarrassed to knock or draw attention to myself, I walked out tentatively into the Shanghai streets. Surely, if I tried hard enough, I would remember the way home.

It was a beautiful, sunny afternoon. At first I **wandered** along a wide, straight road lined with tall, leafy trees. Motor cars, trams, rickshaws, pedicabs and bicycles **whizzed** by. I kept walking but dared not cross the road, glancing briefly at the open-fronted stores overhung with colourful, upright, bilingual signboards. I turned a corner and now the pavements **seethed** with people and noise and commotion: labourers shouldering heavy loads on bamboo poles; hawkers selling toys, crickets in cages, fans, cold tea, candies, meat-filled buns, spring rolls, tea-eggs and fermented bean curd; stalls and booths offering services such as hair-cuts, shaves, dental care, letter-writing, extraction of ear wax; beggars banging tin cups and chanting for a handout. Except for me, everyone was striding along purposefully, going somewhere. Everyone had a destination. I must have walked for miles and miles. But where was I?

Should I enter a shop and ask for directions? But I didn't know my home address. What should I say? Should I approach that kindly old storekeeper smiling at me from the doorway of his antique shop and tell him, 'Please, sir, I want to go home'? But where *was* my home?

I walked past a bustling, brightly lit *dim sum* shop. Such a wonderful aroma was wafting through the door! Through the plate-glass window, I saw roast ducks, soya-sauce chickens, and hunks of glistening meat hanging from hooks. There was a young chef wielding his cleaver and deftly chopping a duck into bite-sized pieces on a wooden block. Wouldn't it be heavenly to be given a slice of meat? But that might be too much to hope for. I would be quite content with a piece of bone to chew on. As I **salivated**, I imagined the taste of the food sliding down my throat. Breakfast seemed such a long time ago!

6 This activity will help you analyse the effect on the reader of Text 5C. Work with a partner.

a How many senses have been used in the description in Text 5C? Give examples of each.

b The aim of the passage is to create a sense of exclusion and loneliness. Which images or ideas did you find the most powerful? Can you explain why?

c Look at the following verbs which are in bold in the passage. Say what you associate with each of them, and how they contribute to the effectiveness of the description. (You may need to check the meaning of some of them.)

clanged   wandered   whizzed   seethed   salivated

d Look at the use of the following stylistic devices in the passage and collect examples of each. Then comment on the effect of each of them in relation to the content and mood of the passage.
  i   short, simple sentences   iii exclamations
  ii questions   iv lists

e How is sympathy for Adeline created in this passage?

7 a Study the photograph below very closely. Jot down words and phrases which come into your mind, using a mind map divided into the different aspects of the portrait, e.g. eyes, hair.

An old woman from the Zanskar valley in the Himalayas

b Think about the woman's lifestyle and what has made her look this way. Add more ideas to your mind map, including some imagery.

c Decide on the best way to organise a description of the woman. How will you start and finish?

d Write a description of the woman, about one page in length. Choose your words carefully to avoid repetition, making sure your vocabulary is precise and evocative.

e Read your description to the class or give it to your teacher.

The Amish way of life

A lot of people **yearn** for a simpler way of life, a closer relationship with the natural world, and a stronger sense of fellowship with those around them. They are willing to give up the **trappings** of a consumerist society, to live apart from the rest of the world, to **abide** by a strict set of rules, and to work together to build a community.

The artificial communities created by reality TV programmes won't have reached the Amish people of the United States, because they don't have televisions. Even if they did, they wouldn't be able to watch them, because they don't have electricity. Anyway, they are far too busy living that kind of life to be bothered watching other people playing at it.

The Amish people originate from the Anabaptists of 16th-century Switzerland. In the late 17th century they formed their own church, named after their leader, Jacob Amman. They were **persecuted** for their beliefs, so they fled Europe in the mid-18th century to settle in North America, where there are now around 130,000 Amish people, many of them living in Pennsylvania. They speak Pennsylvania Dutch (originally Deutsch), a dialect of German, and their way of life is in many ways unchanged from that of their ancestors, following an unwritten code of **non-conformist** conduct which governs their behaviour.

The Amish work the land using traditional methods rather than modern machinery, and travel by horse-drawn buggy. They make their own clothes, in plain **unadorned** materials, and do not wear make-up or jewellery. Married men grow beards but not moustaches, which have military associations and clash with their **pacifist** outlook. They disapprove of photography or pictures of any kind.

The Amish have an age-old practice of barn-raising, whereby members of the community come together to build a barn in a day. This is a rare example in today's world of unselfish, brotherly love. Their **no-frills**, back-to-basics way of life has been preserved by such **rituals** and strong, simple rules. Those who break them are **shunned** by the community, and readmitted only after a period of repentance.

Work with a partner to study aspects of Text 5D in Activities 8 and 9.

8 a Give the part of speech and meaning for each of the ten words in bold in Text 5D.

  b Think of headings which would summarise the content of each of the five paragraphs of the passage.

  c What is the attitude of the author to the subject of the article? Find examples to support your inference.

9 a Using a copy of Text 5D and with your partner, circle all the connectives used in the passage. How many different ones are there?

  b Look at the sentence structures in the first paragraph of the passage. How would you describe them?

  c Rewrite paragraph four of the passage (starting 'The Amish work the land …') using the same structural device. Use the tip below to help you.

Tip

For Activity 9c
Parallel structures

If there are several related and equally weighted pieces of information to give about a subject, a kind of listing device can be used which puts them together as parallel structures linked only by a comma, and an *and* or *or* before the last item in the list. They have the same grammatical structure, often beginning with the infinitive, as in the second sentence of Text 5D. This device gives balance, elegance and fluency to the writing. Like everything else, however, it should be used sparingly so that the overall piece has variety.

Text 5E

A 19-year-old from the UK describes her typical day.

My secret life as a teen detective

When I can be bothered, I get up at 7 and go for a swim. But I won't lie – that doesn't happen every day. Anyway, at 8 o'clock my iPod is set to play my favourite song, and that wakes me up.

I live with my mum, my brother and three foster sisters in a tiny village in Surrey. I work for a company called Answers Investigation. The office is in the middle of nowhere. I turn up for work, never knowing if I'll be leaving at 5 or at midnight, or if I'll be on a train to somewhere at noon. I love working crazy hours; it's better than being bored, sat in a 9-to-5 kind of job. I had no idea a job like this was real, but I always liked the thought of being some top-secret spy.

In the office, I check my emails and Facebook. I make coffees for the guys and green tea for myself. There are three of us full time – me, Andy and Nigel – plus we have specialists and part-time investigators all over the place.

When it comes to undercover work there are roles that only a teen detective can do. I can act young *and* mature. I've been a 14-year-old, a college student, an office worker, a ditsy idiot – people will tell you anything if they think you're stupid – as well as some randomer on a train who you would never know was following you. Acting is what makes me tick.

For surveillance operations we prepare for every possible scenario, but people always surprise you, so you have to stay focused. Sitting in my car for 12 hours is never fun. I prefer surveillance when it's active, like once when I tailed a guy around London – I was five steps behind him the entire day. He never noticed. We trace people from the office too, using databases and social-networking sites. It's harder if they're over 50, but if they're under 20 it's easy as pie; it's so bad the stupid things people put about themselves online.

I've been in situations with all sorts of criminals. But when I'm undercover with a dodgy person I'm never on my own. And I have a distress signal – I tie my hair up – as people I know are in eyeshot at all times. I use a voice recorder and a camera, with the look and size of a button, attached to my handbag.

My life is peachy. But of course you get affected by things on the job. You learn to move on and remember the reasons why you're doing it. Getting a good result for a client is the best feeling ever – like the case when, after months of trawling, we helped a man who was adopted to track down his birth mother in Spain. And we helped a Saudi father protect his daughter by exposing her fiancé's dodgy financial dealings. Our investigators have travelled to Dubai, France, Ibiza . . .

I see my friends when I can. Otherwise, the responsibility with my job makes me completely crash out in the evenings. I need to watch television or read a book in order to switch off. I like magic, fairy stories, things that aren't real.

Sunday Times Magazine

10 a The following words from Text 5E are often misspelt. Write them out with their 'hot spots' underlined. Then see if you can write them correctly without looking.

    college   surveillance   scenario   surprise   affected

b Rewrite paragraph three of the passage, joining the sentences with connectives and using participle phrases to make one complex sentence. How many different ways can it be done?

c The passage represents an oral genre and contains colloquial and idiomatic phrases. Replace those below with standard English:

i	can be bothered	ix	I tailed a guy
ii	in the middle of nowhere	x	it's easy as pie
iii	working crazy hours	xi	a dodgy person
iv	sat in a 9-to-5 kind of job	xii	are in eyeshot
v	me, Andy and Nigel	xiii	my life is peachy
vi	all over the place	xiv	months of trawling
vii	a ditsy idiot	xv	crash out
viii	what makes me tick	xvi	switch off

11 Work in small groups on these writing activities.

a Write a newspaper advertisement for the job of private investigator with Answers Investigation, using information from Text 5E. Look at the tip to help you.

For Activity 11a
Job advertisements

Job advertisements are brief, as words cost money and the key information needs to be conveyed in the most concise way possible. They mention the character qualities and academic or other qualifications which a successful applicant should have, and explain the rewards, challenges and working conditions which go with the job. Finally, a deadline date is given for the application, and an address to which it should be sent. You can begin your advertisement with 'Wanted . . .'

b Write the CV (curriculum vitae or résumé) for a suitable applicant for the job. Use the tip on the next page for guidance.

Tip

For Activity 11b
CVs

A CV tells a prospective employer everything they need to know about a job applicant. It begins with the applicant's full name, address and other contact details. Then there follows, expressed very concisely, a summary of the applicant's relevant experience so far. If the applicant is still at school then the subjects they are studying and the exam passes they have already gained or are expected to gain would be given. Hobbies and personal interests may also be mentioned, and any useful accomplishments, such as having passed a driving test or done a self-defence course.

c   Write the letter of application for the job, addressed to the personnel manager at Answers Investigation. Then give your CV and letter to your teacher, who will judge which group produced the best of each and which candidate would be most likely to get the job.

Key point

Formal letter writing

The usual formula for a formal letter is three paragraphs: the first to explain the reason for writing and the general situation; the second to give background details and further relevant information about the topic or issue; the final one to explain what you would like the result of your letter to be. One side of typed writing is the expected length.

If you know the name of the person you are writing to, you can address them as 'Dear Mr/Mrs/Ms' + name, and sign yourself with your full name after 'Yours sincerely'. If you do not know the name of the recipient then you must use either 'Dear Sir/Madam' or their official position, e.g. Editor, Headteacher, and sign with your initials and surname after 'Yours faithfully'.

In the case of a job application letter: refer in the first paragraph to when and where you saw the advertisement and mention the accompanying CV; explain in the second paragraph why you want the job and what you have to offer the company; say in the third paragraph that you hope they will look favourably upon your application, that you are willing to provide any further information, and that you look forward to being invited for an interview.

12 You are going to write a description of a person you see often in your neighbourhood while they are doing their job, such as a local shopkeeper or bus driver. You can make use of ideas and devices you have looked at during your study of this unit, for example those referred to in Activity 6.

a Plan three paragraphs which focus on:
  i physical appearance
  ii personality
  iii how they do their job.

b Add specific details to your plan, and make your language both informative and evocative, using imagery.

c Write about a page of description, then check it and give it to your teacher.

UNIT 6 The race

In this unit you will read for implicit meaning, and look at the importance of structure, style and viewpoint when describing an event. The writing activities include a diary entry, a news article, a narrative extension and a short story, and you will also do further vocabulary, grammar, punctuation and spelling practice.

Activities

1   **a**   Contribute to a list on the board of all the different kinds of race you can think of.

     b   Discuss and decide on ways of grouping them by category.

     c   Share with a partner an account of a personal experience of either participating in or being a spectator at a memorable race.

Text 6A is about a famous horse race held in a town in Italy. The prepositions have been removed.

Text 6A

The Palio di Siena

The world-famous *Palio di Siena* is a horse race held twice each year, [1] _____ 2nd July and 16th August, [2] _____ Siena, Italy. The celebrated race dates back [3] _____ medieval times; the costumes and banners belong [4] _____ the middle ages.

Ten costumed horses and bareback riders, dressed [5] _____ the appropriate colours, represent ten of the seventeen *contrade*, or city wards. There is insufficient space [6] _____ all seventeen *contrade* to take part [7] _____ the Palio [8] _____ any one occasion. A magnificent pageant precedes the race, which attracts visitors and spectators [9] _____ around the world.

The horses are [10] _____ mixed breed; no purebred horses are allowed. The race itself takes place in the town's central square, the Piazza del Campo, [11] _____ which a thick layer of dirt has been laid, and where the corners are protected [12] _____ padded crash barriers. The race consists [13] _____ three circuits and usually lasts no more than 90 seconds. It is not uncommon for a few of the jockeys to be thrown [14] _____ their horses while making the treacherous turns in the piazza, or to see unmounted horses finishing the race [15] _____ their jockeys.

The detonation of an explosive charge echoes [16] _____ the piazza, signalling [17] _____ the thousands of onlookers that the race is about to begin. [18] _____ the dangerous, steeply angled track, the riders are allowed to use their whips not only [19] _____ their own horse, but also [20] _____ disturbing other horses and riders. They are allowed to push and distract each other. The Palio's winner is the horse which represents his *contrada*, and not the jockey – a riderless horse can win. The victor is awarded a banner of painted silk, or *palio*, which is hand-painted [21] _____ a different artist for each race.

There may be some danger [22] _____ spectators from the sheer number of people [23] _____ attendance. The enthusiasm [24] _____ followers after the victory is extreme, and there are occasional outbreaks of violence [25] _____ partisans of rival *contrade*, who regard this as not just a simple horse race but a matter for traditional passion and pride passed down the generations.

2 Using a copy of Text 6A, work with a partner to fill in the gaps and study the vocabulary of the passage.

a Insert the 25 missing prepositions.

b Now look at the words *pageant* and *generations*. List other words you can think of which need to be spelt with an *e* after a *g*. Read the key point on the next page to help you.

Key point

Spelling and pronunciation concerning the letter *g*

Without a following *e* or *i*, the letter *g* is usually pronounced hard, as in *tango, gutter* and *regret*. Where the *g* is the initial letter, a *u* is often inserted to preserve the hard *g*, as in *guess*, which would otherwise be pronounced like a *j*, as in *gesture*. Notice that in *ageing, management* and *changeable* the *e* of the verb form has been retained to keep the soft *g*.

c Find and list the ten words in the passage which mean the same as the following:

i of the middle ages	iv partisans	vii dangerous	ix onlookers
ii famous	v riders	viii riderless	x winner
iii dressed up	vi disturb		

a Write a one-paragraph entry for an encyclopedia to explain what the *Palio di Siena* is.

b Write a short description of the *Palio di Siena* to be used as an advertisement to attract visitors to the spectacle.

c Write a diary entry as a spectator of the event which sets the scene and explains what happened during the race.

Tip

For Activity 3c
Writing a diary entry

Use references to what the senses are experiencing in order to create the atmosphere of a large crowd waiting excitedly for a much looked-forward-to and dangerous event. Describe the people and their appearance and behaviour, as well as the place and the action of the race. Remember that diaries mention not only events and descriptions but also thoughts, feelings and possibly speech, if relevant and dramatic. In this case you could include what people are shouting to the riders.

Text 6B

File   Edit   View   History   Bookmarks   Help

Lightning Bolt gunning for 9.4 as sprint king vows to smash 100 m world record in London

Triple Olympic champion Usain Bolt aims to 'amaze' the world at London 2012 by running 9.4 seconds for the 100 m and 19 seconds for the 200 m.

Jamaican Bolt, 25, is the reigning Olympic champion and world-record holder over both distances, with times of 9.58 secs and 19.19 secs.

'People are looking forward to me running 9.4, 19 seconds, anything that's amazing,' Bolt told BBC Sport. Bolt's 9.58 secs 100 m world record was set at the 2009 World Championships in Berlin.

He told BBC1 programme *100 Days To Go* that more performances such as the ones that saw him take three gold medals at the 2008 Olympics in Beijing would make him 'a living legend'.

'They want to see my personality, me enjoying it and doing crazy stuff, but they also want to see that time,' he said.

'If I dominate the Olympics, I'll be a living legend. A living legend walking around. Sounds good.

'I'm working as hard as possible so I can go as fast as possible.'

www.dailymail.co.uk/sport/

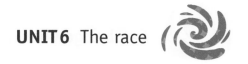

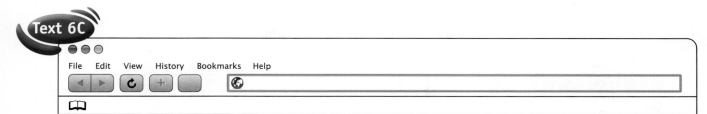

| File | Edit | View | History | Bookmarks | Help |

Usain Bolt's Olympic 100 m triumph triggers jubilation in Jamaica

Usain Bolt's 100 metres Olympic victory sparked ecstatic celebrations in his homeland, where national pride was already riding high on the eve of celebrations to mark 50 years of Jamaica's independence.

Unbridled joy from crowds gathered in the centre of Kingston grew louder with every second as the powerful strides of the world's fastest man took him to the finish line.

Bolt's early birthday present to his country, delivered in a blistering 9.63 seconds, was exactly what hundreds, including many who had journeyed from the sprinter's parish of Trelawny, had come to watch together on a big screen. Traffic in the Jamaican capital came to a standstill as people, braving the cold and rain of tropical storm Ernesto, sounded horns and clanged pot covers.

Others mimicked the now famous pose of the double Olympic champion or cheered each appearance of his compatriot Yohan Blake, who many considered as Bolt's main rival going into the race but who finished a respectable second with a time of 9.75 seconds.

The passion was just as great closer to the scene of Bolt's historic feat last night at the Jamaica House – a bit of the Caribbean island created at the North Greenwich Arena, London, which has operated as a base for Jamaican fans.

Bolt triggered an endless blanket of noise and hysteria. The moment the gun was fired, the crowd chanted and brayed and hooted and they didn't stop until he was safely home.

'I am so happy,' said Rosa Nelson, 37, from Edmonton, north London, pausing to mimic Bolt's trademark archery stance. 'He represents a small nation, the best of our small nation presenting itself to the world. We have the fastest man and the fastest woman. We are confident and we are proud and now we are even prouder.'

Saturday's 100 metre gold retention by Jamaican Shelly-Ann Fraser-Pryce was a source of pride, but it was just the start. The desire for a country of just 2.9 million people to be recognised as unassailable – if only on the 100 metre track – required total victory in the men's event.

In the Kingston crowd, Mark Green said, 'Let me tell you this, he is the best, none of them can touch him. We are so proud right now. Happy Jamaica 50.'

www.guardian.co.uk/sport

File   Edit   View   History   Bookmarks   Help

Bolt's heartland of Sherwood Content erupts in celebration

'A yah so nice!'

Sherwood Content, Trelawny, Jamaica – Wild celebrations broke out across this small community after their most celebrated native, Usain Bolt, finished ahead of a strong field in the 100 metres final at the London Olympics yesterday.

'To the world! I am on top of the world. I am floating,' Bolt's aunt Lillian Bolt exclaimed in jubilation shortly after the race.

'From I see him move out in the heats I say yes, he is ready. And the semi-finals . . . gosh man he was there. He delivered,' she said.

When her flesh and blood blew away the field in a quick 9.63 seconds for an Olympic record, Lillian broke out into wild celebration, dancing to the beat of the reggae song 'Bolt', which was recorded after the phenomenal sprinter's victory at the Olympics in Beijing, China, four years ago.

Bolt's uncle Andrew Davis said he was confident that his nephew would better the field, especially following his effortless performance in the two qualifying races leading up to the final.

'I was not thinking he would have lowered his world record, but with the ease and comfort with which he did the heats and semis, I knew he would win convincingly,' an elated Davis said.

Meanwhile, Lillian, who watched the race from her house, was joined shortly after by cheering members of the community, mostly decked out in the black, green and gold national colours, some beating pot covers, singing and dancing.

However, the celebration was not confined to Sherwood Content as a spontaneous motorcade wormed from the community into Falmouth, the parish capital, 15 kilometres away.

'A so the ting go, a yah so nice,' one cheerful supporter was heard shouting in the historic Water Square in Falmouth.

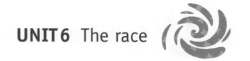

'Lightning strike twice,' another jubilant supporter shouted as he mimicked Bolt's famous To The World pose.

In the meantime, Lillian says her nephew is without a doubt a track and field legend now.

She also argued that Bolt's first-place finish and Yohan Blake's runner-up performance in the race, which followed Shelly-Ann Fraser-Pryce's gold, and Veronica Campbell Brown's bronze over a similar distance in the women's 100 metres on Saturday, set the tone for the nation's 50th year of independence.

Lillian called upon the government to consider Bolt as a national treasure.

www.jamaicaobserver.com/sport

4 **a** After reading Texts 6B, 6C and 6D, summarise in one sentence what Usain Bolt wanted to achieve and did achieve in the 2012 London Olympics.

b Comment on the differences of headline of the three news reports.

c Comment on any differences you can find in the style and content of the three reports.

5 You are going to write a news article, using material from Texts 6B, 6C and 6D. Use the tip below to help you.

a Collect information from the three texts as notes, ignoring any repetition of ideas or quotations.

b Put numbers against the notes to show the best order in which to use them.

c Write the combined article in your own words and an appropriate style, and give it a new title of your own.

For Activity 5
News articles

Texts 6B, 6C and 6D are news reports. A news article may contain more opinions and personal viewpoints than a news report. The main difference is that it is not linked to any particular event which has just occurred but gives a wider picture of a current situation. Like a news report, however, an article usually mentions the immediate context first, followed by background information, and it includes details and quotations. The title of an article will give a general indication of its content but not be as specific as a news report headline. For instance, 'Jamaica is celebrating' could be a title for a news article, whereas 'Bolt wins 100 metres' is more likely to be a news report headline.

Text 6E is a short story about motor racing. You will give it your own title.

Rory felt the heat rising off the road surface in front of his car. A trickle of sweat ran down his face under his multi-coloured helmet. Thoughts of the other challengers flitted through his head as he waited for the signal to start. He knew most of them from previous meetings. Chuck and Glen were both competitive, although he was confident he had the edge on them with his new motor. It was the new drivers from the country meetings that he was unsure of.

There was concentration on all the faces, spectators and drivers alike, as they waited for the starter's instructions. A crackling speaker signalled imminent action. 'Drivers start your engines.'

A deafening sound of revving motors filled the air. Cars sped off, weaving from side to side in an effort to heat the tyres during the warm-up lap. Confident in his ability to beat this field, Rory charged forward as the starter's car moved off the track and the green light flashed for them to start. Rory forgot everything as the thrill of speed and power from the V8 engine under his bonnet took over. The track had been watered to keep the dust down. It had now turned into mud. Red dirt caked on the wheels and flicked up onto his windscreen, blurring his vision as he sped up beside Chuck, who had forged ahead of him. In an attempt to keep him out Rory over-corrected. A sudden bash from the rear shunted him to the left and he was annoyed.

'So you want to play rough, eh! I'll show you what happens when you pick on me.' Within seconds he shunted one of the new boys sideways. This set up a chain reaction. Cars collided and ricocheted off one another. Somewhere during the ensuing laps he noticed Chuck's car wedged backwards into the

fence. With adrenaline pumping, the race ended in a mighty drag for the finish against the new boy, who had more power under his bonnet than Rory had expected. Today, luck was with him; he had held the new driver off, with Jim finishing a close third.

In the pits, Rory headed towards the new driver's car. Offering his hand he said, 'Not bad. You put up quite a challenge. Rory Carter is the name.' Accepting the outstretched hand but not meeting Rory's gaze, the driver nodded. 'Yeah, if she'd been firing on all six you wouldn't have stood a chance. I'm Lee Grange.' 'Come on, don't blame your motor. You were flat out,' Rory scoffed.

Lee squared his shoulders, and then lifted the bonnet. 'That's what you think. Take a look under here.'

'You're right, the lead's off. What have you got in that thing?'

'If I told you, I might not get my own back next time.'

'Yeah, yeah.' Rory glanced over the bodywork. 'You don't advertise any sponsors, so who does your work?'

Lee smiled, 'You're looking at it. That's why I didn't make it for the other races; I had a hassle with the starter motor. Now, I've got work to do.' With that Lee slid through the window into the driving seat. The engine spurted into life and the car drove from the pits in a haze of red dust.

*   *   *   *   *   *

True to his word, Lee made Rory eat his dust in every race at their next meeting a few weeks later. Rory had expected to find Lee waiting to gloat and was surprised that neither he nor his car were anywhere in the pits.

He didn't understand the guy. Most drivers couldn't resist the chance to brag after beating him, yet Lee didn't even hang around to accept his trophy.

A week later, Rory was in the wrecking yard chasing a few parts when Lee walked around one of the wrecks.

'Because you won this time don't expect to beat me every week,' Rory laughed.

'We'll see what happens, eh?' Lee challenged back.

'What is it with you? I try to be friendly and make conversation, yet you act as though . . .'

Lee pulled his hood further forward. 'I grew up on a farm, helping Dad on anything with an engine. I guess I'm sort of a loner and my stubbornness stems from that.'

'That explains the mechanical skill, but where does the racing come into it?'

'From watching my brother race around the paddocks, I suppose. He never let me have a go in case Mum caught us.'

'Why could your brother do it and not you?'

'I suppose it was because I was the youngest, and you know what mothers are like. So let's drop it. OK?'

Rory couldn't understand this guy; something niggled at him.

'I'll see you at the next meeting.'

'Sure.'

*   *   *   *   *   *

Rory won the first two races and Lee won the next two. Each time he saw Lee he felt more curious. It frustrated him more when Lee didn't show for the next two meetings. Then Rory missed the following meeting himself through work commitments. He had to deliver a car to Bunbury and pick up an exchange one for his father's car yard. While there, he decided to check out the local speedway.

'No, it can't be!' he muttered, as a blue car flashed past with 65 painted on the side. 'Why on earth would Lee be racing down here?' he asked himself. He watched him jockey for position from the middle of the pack. One by one he picked them off. Fifth, fourth, third. Suddenly the first and second cars clashed. Lee's car was shunted sideways and clipped the fence. Fifth tried to avoid him, but instead spun him round, lifting and spinning him end for end along the fence.

Time stood still for Rory. He saw the orange sparks fly through the night air when it clipped the power pole. Concern for Lee moved his legs into action. Pushing people out of the way, he jumped over the fence and ran to the battered driver's side door. He ripped the torn webbing from its clips in an effort to help Lee.

Rory panicked at the sight of blood where Lee's leathers had been ripped. Fumbling, he undid his helmet.

'OK, let us in,' came the order from a paramedic. Pushed out of the way, Rory hovered nearby as Lee's unconscious body was placed onto the stretcher and carried into the ambulance.

Fighting back a bevy of mixed emotions, Rory rushed to follow the ambulance, the vision of long golden hair stamped on his mind, and her perfume still lingering.

Eileen Hughes

6 **a** Give the short story in Text 6E a title. It should be brief and appropriate, and not give away the ending.

  b Write one sentence to explain the social issue raised in the story.

  c Write one sentence to explain the irony in the story.

7 With a partner, discuss the following questions about Text 6E, then feed back to the class.

  a How would the story have been different if Lee had been the narrator and not Rory?

  b What do you think would have happened in the story if it had continued?

  c What is the reader supposed to think and feel after reading the story?

8 **a** Jot down some notes about different kinds of races and how they might end. You could discuss your ideas with a partner.

  b Choose which one you want to write about, and think of two or three characters to include, and where the race will take place.

  c Plan a short story called 'The Race' and write the first paragraph. Read the tip on the next page to help you.

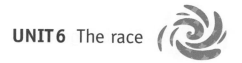

For Activity 8c
Planning a short story

It is important to choose a viewpoint which is going to achieve the effect you are aiming for, which may be an ironic twist, pathos (pity) or humour. The main character needs to be established in the opening paragraph. If you choose a first person persona, then you need to include information which tells the reader who this person is.

You can start your story, as Text 6E does, in the middle of the action to immediately engage the reader. Descriptive skill is important in writing narrative because without enough detail to be able to envisage the scene and identify with the character a narrative will not be engaging or effective.

You must know how a story is going to end before you begin it so that the clues can be left which will make the ending plausible, though not obvious. You also need to keep up the pace and suspense – and keep to an appropriate length – which means you must decide which details and events to include and which to leave out because they are unnecessary.

Text 6F is a modern retelling and extension of an Ancient Greek fable.

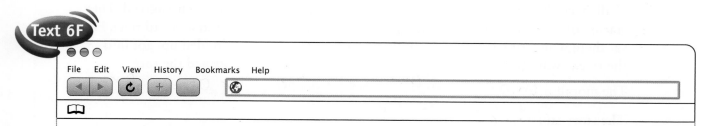

Ancient Greek fable: The race of the hare and the tortoise

Once upon a time a tortoise and a hare had an argument about who was faster. They decided to settle the argument with a race. They agreed on a route and started off. The hare shot ahead and ran briskly for some time. Then seeing that he was far ahead of the tortoise, he thought he'd relax before continuing the race. He sat under a tree and soon fell asleep. The tortoise, plodding on, overtook him and finished the race, emerging as the undisputed champion. The hare woke up and realised that he'd lost.

The moral: *Slow and steady wins the race.*

But the story doesn't end here!
The hare was disappointed at losing the race and he did some soul-searching. He realised that he'd lost the race only because he had been over-confident and careless. If he had not taken things for granted, there's no way the tortoise could have beaten him. So he challenged the tortoise to another race.

The tortoise agreed. This time, the hare went all out and ran without stopping from start to finish. He won by several kilometres.

The moral: _Confidence is key in moderation_

But the story doesn't end here!
The tortoise did some thinking this time, and realised that there's no way a tortoise could beat a hare in a race the way it was currently designed. So he challenged the hare to another race, but over a different route. The hare agreed. They started off. The hare took off and ran at top speed until he came to a broad river. He sat there wondering what to do. In the meantime the tortoise plodded up, got into the river, swam to the opposite bank, continued walking and finished the race.

The moral: _things might be easier for others from your point of view_

The story still hasn't ended!
The hare and the tortoise, by this time, had become good friends and they did some thinking together. They decided to rerun the last race, but as a team this time. They started off, and this time the hare carried the tortoise until the riverbank. There, the tortoise took over and swam across with the hare on his back. On the opposite bank, the hare again carried the tortoise and they reached the finishing line together. They both felt a greater sense of satisfaction than they'd felt earlier.

The moral: _team work makes the dream work_

Sonnie Santos

9 In small groups, discuss the story in Text 6F.

a Discuss and agree on the three morals to insert at the end of the three extra stages to the story. Write them in your notebook.

b Discuss and agree on a modern version of this extended fable (e.g. based on a situation which occurs in a school or workplace).

c Divide the different stages of your version between the group members to write them and read them to the class.

Text 6G is a passage from a book by a journalist-photographer about unusual sports in Asia. It describes a donkey race in Karachi, Pakistan.

We drove off to find the best viewing spot, which turned out to be the crest of the hill so we could see the approaching race. I asked the lads if we could join in the 'Wacky Races' and follow the donkeys, and they loved the idea. 'We'll open the car boot, you climb inside and point your camera towards the race. As the donkeys overtake us, we'll join the cars.' 'But will you try and get to the front?' 'Oh yes, that's no problem.'

The two lads who had never been interested in this Karachi sport were suddenly fired up with enthusiasm. We waited for an eternity on the brow of the hill, me perched in the boot with a zoom lens pointing out. Nearly one hour later I was beginning to feel rather silly when there had been no action *apart from* a villager on a wobbly bicycle, who nearly fell off as he cycled past and gazed around at us.

Several vehicles went past, and some donkey-carts carrying spectators. 'Are they coming?' we called out to them. 'Coming, coming,' came the reply. We were beginning to lose faith in its happening, *except for* the lads, who remained confident.

Just as I was assuming that the race had been cancelled, we spotted two

approaching donkey-carts in front of a cloud of fumes and dust created by some fifty vehicles roaring in their wake. As they drew nearer, Yaqoob <u>revved</u> up the engine and began to inch the car out of the lay-by. The two donkeys were almost <u>dwarfed</u> by their **entourage**; but there was no denying their speed. The two were neck-and-neck, their jockeys perched on top of the tiny carts using their whips energetically, although not cruelly.

The noise of the approaching vehicles grew: horns tooting; bells ringing; the special rattles used just for this purpose (like maracas, a metal container filled with dried beans). Men standing on top of their cars and vans, hanging out of taxis and perched on lorries, all cheered and shouted, while the vehicles jostled to get to the front of the <u>convoy</u>.

Yaqoob chose exactly the right moment to edge out of the road and swerve in front of the nearest car, finding the perfect place to see the two donkeys and at the front of the vehicles. This was Formula One without rules, or a city-centre rush hour gone **anarchic**; a complete **flouting** of every type of traffic rule and common sense.

Our young driver **relished** this unusual test of driving skills. It was survival of the fittest, and depended upon the ability to cut in front of a vehicle with a sharp flick of the steering wheel (no lane discipline here); quick **reflexes** to spot a gap in the traffic for a couple of seconds; nerves of steel, and an effective horn. There were two races – the motorised spectators at the back; in front, the two donkeys, still running close and amazingly not put off by the **uproar** just behind them. Ahead of the donkeys, oncoming traffic – for it was a main road – had to dive into the ditch and wait there until we had passed. Yaqoob loved it. We stayed near the front, his hand permanently on the horn.

The road straightened and levelled, and everyone picked up speed as we neared the end of the race. But just as they were reaching the finishing line, the hospital gate, there was a near pile-up as the leading donkey swerved, lost his footing and he and the cart tumbled. The race was over.

And then the trouble began. I assumed the winner was the one who completed the race but it was not seen that way by everyone. *Apart from* the two jockeys and 'officials' (who, it turned out, were actually **monitoring** the race) there were over a hundred spectators who all had strong opinions on the outcome. Some were claiming that the donkey had fallen because the other one had been ridden too close to him. Voices were raised, tempers were rising, and many were trying to insist that the race should be re-run.

> Yaqoob and Iqbal were nervous of hanging around a **volatile** situation. They agreed to find out for me what was happening, ordering me to stay inside the car as they were swallowed up by the crowd. They emerged some time later. 'It's still not **resolved**,' said Iqbal, 'but there's no point hanging around. I think we should leave.' As we drove away, Yaqoob reflected on his driving skills. 'I really enjoyed that,' he said as we drove off at a more **sedate** pace. 'But I don't even have my licence yet because I'm underage!'
>
> *From* A Game of Polo with a Headless Goat *by Emma Levine*

10 Discuss the following questions as a class.

   a What did you enjoy about Text 6G? Give examples.

   b How do you think this passage differs from Text 6E?

   c How do you think the account has been made humorous?

11 **a** Give synonyms, in the context and in the same part of speech, for the ten words in bold in Text 6G.

i	entourage	**iv**	relished	**vii**	monitoring	**ix** resolved
ii	anarchic	**v**	reflexes	**viii**	volatile	**x** sedate
iii	flouting	**vi**	uproar			

   b Use the following five words, which are underlined in the passage, in sentences which show that you understand their meaning.

      perched   zoom   revved   dwarfed   convoy

   c The five words below, which are in red in the passage, are homonyms (they have the same spelling and pronunciation but can have a different meaning from that in the passage). Write five sentences to illustrate their other meaning. They may be in a different part of speech.

      crest   boot   brow   wake   edge

12 **a** There are places in Text 6G where a new line should have been started for a change of speaker. On a copy of Text 6G, mark // where the new lines are needed.

   b On a copy of Text 6G circle the semi-colons. How are they being used? How does this compare with what you learnt about them in Unit 3 and Unit 5?

   c Both *except for* and *apart from* are in italics in the passage. Find the three uses and work out the rule for how they are used. Write a sentence for each. Read the tip on the next page if you need help.

Tip

For Activity 12c
Except for and *apart from*

Except for means 'not including' and is therefore always used to exclude or subtract (e.g. 'They were all there except for Mary').
Apart from can mean both 'not including' and 'in addition to' (e.g. 'There was no one there apart from Mary'; 'Apart from Mary, there were three others there'). When *apart from* is being used to show addition, it normally comes at the beginning of the sentence. *Besides* can be used instead of *apart from* to indicate an addition, and can come after (e.g. 'There were three others there besides Mary').

13 a The following words from Text 6G are tricky to spell. Write them out with their 'hot spots' underlined and notice what makes them difficult. Then cover the words and write them correctly.

enthusiasm   vehicles   energetically   jostled   discipline

b What do you notice about the following words?

cancelled   levelled   medallist   travelled   jewellery   metallic

c Can you see a pattern in the spelling of these words, and think of a reason for it?

Key point

Doubling the *l*

In verbs of two syllables ending in a short vowel followed by an *l*, we double the *l* (except in American English) when a suffix is added, whatever part of speech they are. As an exception, verbs ending in *ol*, pronounced as a long vowel, also have double *l*, as in *controlled*. This rule also applies to many verbs ending in *t* when they are given a suffix (e.g. *admitted*, *regretting*). It is similar to the rule about when consonants need to be doubled. If the words in the list in Activity 13b had only a single *l*, the preceding vowel would be pronounced long rather than short, as it is in *regaled* and *competed*.

14 With a partner, discuss the vocabulary and aspects of the style of Text 6G.

a Generally, how would you describe the type of vocabulary used in Text 6G, and what is the effect?

b Generally, how would you describe the type of sentences used in the passage, and what is the effect?

c There are clichés (overused/predictable expressions) in the passage because it is journalistic not literary writing. Find ten examples.

15 Plan and write a short story which includes an account of a race, after reading the tip below.

For Activity 15
Writing a short story

You could continue the story you planned and began in Activity 8, or plan and write another one using Text 6G as a model. Begin with the introduction of the setting and characters before the event, in order to put the reader in the picture and create anticipation.

- Even accounts intending to be informative will exaggerate the facts and use sensational language and references to the senses to create drama and entertain the reader. Notice how strong the sense of sound is in Text 6G.

- Think about the best type of vocabulary and sentence structures to use for your particular story and the effect you want to create.

- Avoid clichés in your story so that the reader is more engaged by the language. Overused similes and metaphors do not evoke a strong response from the reader (e.g. 'nerves of steel' in Text 6G). Your figurative language must, however, be appropriate, otherwise the comparison suggested will not be convincing.

- Try to avoid repetition of ideas and references to objects; where these are necessary, use synonyms, as illustrated in both Texts 6A and 6G.

- Think about whether to use some direct speech to add to the drama, as in Texts 6E and 6G.

- Notice in Text 6G how most of the sentences are not only complex but structured in a variety of ways with different beginnings. Some of them delay the key words and idea – using parentheses – until later in the sentence for the creation of suspense.

UNIT 7 Time and history

This unit focuses on giving accounts of historical events and processes. You will learn more about prefixes and word order, interpret a timetable and compare poems from different cultures, in addition to writing a news report and a staged description, and thinking about sonnets.

Activities

1　a　What do you think is the purpose of studying history at school?

　　b　Do you think it will ever be possible for humans to travel backwards or forwards through time? Explain your views.

　　c　Draw a personal timeline which records your own history. Exchange it with that of a partner and compare similarities and differences.

For Activity 1c
Making a timeline

A timeline is a horizontal or vertical line which marks off significant points with a label and a date. Think about times when something significant changed in your family, or when you moved home or school. Perhaps you made a new friend, took up a new hobby or sport, learnt a new skill, or travelled somewhere memorable. A timeline is a personal history and no two are the same, even though external events and public history concern everyone.

Howard Carter was an archeologist who, after years of searching in the pharaohs' burial ground in the Valley of the Kings in Luxor, Egypt, finally made a momentous discovery. Text 7A is adapted from his account of the excavation.

Finding the boy king

Most <u>excavators</u> would confess to a feeling of awe when they break into a chamber closed and sealed many centuries ago. With trembling hands I made a tiny breach in the upper left-hand corner of the sealed

94

doorway. Darkness and blank space, as far as an iron testing-rod could reach, showed that whatever lay beyond was empty. Candle tests were applied as a <u>precaution</u> against possible foul gases and then, widening the hole a little, I inserted the candle and peered in, the others standing anxiously beside me to hear the verdict.

At first I could see nothing, the hot air escaping from the chamber causing the candle flame to flicker, but presently, as my eyes grew accustomed to the light, details of the room within emerged slowly from the mist, strange animals, statues and gold – everywhere the glint of gold. For the moment – an eternity it must have seemed to the others standing by – I was struck dumb with amazement, and when Lord Carnarvon, unable to stand the suspense any longer, inquired anxiously: 'Can you see anything?' it was all I could do to get out the words: 'Yes, wonderful things.'

Then, widening the hole a little further, so that we could both see, we inserted an electric torch. We were simultaneously filled with the exhilaration of discovery, the fever of suspense. Surely never before in the whole history of excavation had such an amazing sight been seen as the light of our torch revealed to us. A roomful – a whole museumful – of objects piled one upon another in seemingly endless profusion.

Presently it dawned upon our bewildered brains that in all this medley before us there was no coffin or trace of a mummy. The explanation gradually dawned. Between the two black sentinel statues there was another sealed doorway. What we saw was merely an <u>antechamber</u> – behind there were to be other chambers, possibly a succession of them, and in one of them, in all his magnificent panoply of death, we should find the pharaoh lying.

Next morning, we removed the blocking of the doorway and we entered the tomb. Here, packed tightly together in this little chamber, were scores of objects, any of which would have filled us with excitement under ordinary <u>circumstances</u> and been considered ample repayment for a full season's work. None of us was prepared for the astonishing vitality that characterised certain of the objects. All of the larger ones were <u>inscribed</u> with the name of Tutankhamun. While we were still excitedly calling each other from one object to another came a new discovery. Beneath the southern-most couch was a small irregular hole in the wall – yet another sealed doorway and plunderer's hole. Clearly we were not, then, to be the first.

Clearing the objects from the antechamber was like playing a gigantic game of **spillikins**. It was a matter of extreme difficulty to move one object without running serious risk of damaging others. Some were in beautiful condition, others in a most precarious state. It was slow, painful work, and nerve-wracking at that, for one felt all the time a heavy weight of responsibility. Destruction of evidence is so easy and yet so hopelessly irreparable. Seven weeks it took us to clear the antechamber, and thankful we were when it was finished without any disaster.

We were ready at last to penetrate the mystery of the sealed door, and it was with trembling hand that I struck the first blow and carefully chipped away the plaster. When I had made a hole large enough to do so, I inserted a torch. An astonishing sight its light revealed, for there, within a metre of the doorway, stretching as far as one could see and blocking the entrance to the chamber, stood what to all appearance was a solid wall of gold.

Had the thieves penetrated the shrine and disturbed the royal burial? Here, on the eastern end, were the great folding doors, closed and bolted but not sealed, that would answer the question for us. Eagerly we withdrew the ebony bolts, the doors swinging back as if closed only yesterday, and, revealed within, yet another shrine. It had similar bolted doors, but upon them was a seal intact, bearing the name of Tutankhamun and a recumbent jackal over Egypt's nine foes. Henceforth, we knew that within the shrine we should be treading where nobody had entered since the boy-king was laid to rest nearly 3300 years before.

spillikins	game in which players try to pick a stick from a heap without moving any of the others

2 **a** Find ten words in Text 7A which mean the same as the following. Note that they are not in order.

i   judgement   iv mixture   vii unstable   ix joy
ii abundance   v   liveliness viii reclining   x wonder
iii adequate   vi enemies

b List the adverbs and adverbial phrases used in the passage to refer to time and to show the passing of time during the process of the discovery. What can you say about them?

c What is the effect of the use of the following in the passage:
i   the non-sentence (end of paragraph three)
ii the rhetorical question (beginning of the last paragraph)
iii the use of passive verbs throughout the passage?

3 Work with a partner for this activity.

a Look at the dashes used in the second paragraph of Text 7A. Agree how they are being used differently in the first and second sentences.

b The following five words, which are underlined in Text 7A, each have a prefix. Try to work out or remember what the prefixes mean. To help you, think of other words you know which have the same prefix. Then read the key point below.

excavators   **pre**caution   **ante**chamber   **circum**stances   **in**scribed

Key point

Time and place prefixes

The more formal a text is, the more likely it is to contain polysyllabic (multi-syllabled) words which have a prefix. Prefixes come mainly from Greek or Latin. You can usually tell if the word has been given a prefix by taking it away and seeing whether what is left is a recognisable word or part of a word. If the word to which the prefix is being added begins with a certain letter, the prefix may shorten or change slightly, as in *emerge* (*ex* meaning *from* or *out of*) and *irregular* (*in* meaning *not*).

You have already learnt about some negative prefixes, those which make the word mean its opposite, such as *irregular*, and about *re*, meaning *again*. Many of the other prefixes relate to a position in time or space. Knowing the meaning of a prefix can help you to guess correctly the meaning of a word, to spell the word correctly, and to avoid confusion between similar prefixes.

The other ones which are worth learning as pairs of opposites are:

pre – before (time) (e.g. *prepare*)
anti – against (e.g. *anti-war*)
ex – out of (e.g. *extract*)
inter – between (e.g. *international*)
hyper/super – over, beyond
   (e.g. *hyperactive, supermarket*)
ante – before (place or time)
   (e.g. *antechamber*)

post – after (e.g. *postpone*)
pro – for (e.g. *proposal*)
in – into (e.g. *intrude*)
intra – within (e.g. *intranet*)
hypo/sub – below (e.g. *hypothermia, submarine*)
retro – behind (time) (e.g. *retrospect*)

c Look at the sentence structures used in Text 7A, both the order of words and the order of clauses. What do you notice about them? Why do you think this device has been used?

Key point

Delayed word order

Normal word or clause order is sometimes rearranged to delay the revelation of the key information for dramatic effect: for example, in the last sentence of the penultimate paragraph in Text 7A, where the third sentence builds up through parentheses to the final word, *gold*; and the third sentence of the last paragraph, which delays the revelation of the inner shrine. This delaying device, which can be applied to both word order and clause order, is found particularly in older texts, but some genres of modern writing also use it – mini-sagas for instance, as well as poetry – in order to save the important or surprising idea until the last possible moment.

 You are going to write a news report based on Text 7A.

a First draw and label a diagram to indicate the layout of the chambers of the tomb.

b Now write a list of the ten stages, briefly and in your own words, that Carter went through before finally being able to see the shrine.

c Write a brief news report, with a headline, to announce Carter's discoveries.

The age of the fortoise

The mountainous character of the Greek island of Lesbos ensures that driving is a **leisurely** process as you wind through a seemingly endless series of hairpin bends. It is just as well, because the car occasionally has some unusual hazards to **negotiate**. Coming round one corner we were suddenly **confronted** by a large, dome-shaped rock inching its way steadily across our path.

We stopped to inspect and found it wasn't a rock but a living fossil, a creature far more ancient than the Mediterranean, a beast as old as the dinosaurs themselves, which had

chosen that moment to cross our path. It felt like an honour. In fact when this wild tortoise started to emerge from its shell, thrusting out a scrawny neck and pushing paddle-like limbs down on the asphalt to renew its journey, we were touched by a double sense of privilege. It appeared to know we intended no harm, and with that sad, ancient **eloquence** the skeletal head turned in our direction to acknowledge our presence. Then the rock continued on its **imperturbable** course and we were left to reflect on its message.

How can you not be moved by the extraordinary slow-motion world of a tortoise? It seems such a powerful comment on the haste of mankind, particularly the fizzy impatience of our modern lives. Everything about the animal seems to argue less speed. Typical is its **longevity**. Some of the individual giant tortoises found on the Galapagos islands may well survive for several hundred years and be the longest-lived animals on Earth. As a life form tortoises and their close relatives, the turtles, have remained **virtually** unchanged since the Jurassic era, 200 million years ago.

However, tortoises' very slowness has been their **undoing** in the past half-century. They are easy creatures to find and collect, and have featured in human diets for thousands of years. It is probably the release or escape of domestic stock that accounts for their presence on Greek islands. Until a ban was introduced in the 1970s they were routinely sold by French fishmongers. In Bulgaria the last tortoise restaurant closed only in the 1980s.

However, the much more serious problem, along with habitat loss from agricultural intensification, has been collection for the pet trade. In the 1960s and 1970s millions of tortoises were taken from countries all around the Mediterranean. Most of these animals died **prematurely**, largely as a **consequence** of ignorance.

Mark Cocker, Guardian Weekly

 5

a In what ways is the tortoise described in Text 7B like a rock?

b List the reasons why the number of wild tortoises is declining.

c What, in your own words, do you think is the message that the tortoise would want us to reflect on?

The following activities focus on the grammar and vocabulary in Text 7B.

 6

a Without looking back at Text 7B, say what part of speech you think these five words are, judging from the word endings.

steadily   scrawny   skeletal   intensification   ignorance

b Replace the ten words in bold in the passage with synonymous words or phrases. You may have to use a dictionary or thesaurus.

i	leisurely	iv	eloquence	vii	virtually	ix	prematurely
ii	negotiate	v	imperturbable	viii	undoing	x	consequence
iii	confronted	vi	longevity				

c 'We intended *no* harm', in paragraph two of Text 7B, means 'we didn't intend *any* harm'. We also say 'I want *some* information' and 'I don't want *any* information'. What is the rule for when we use *no*, *some* and *any* before a noun? Give other pairs of examples.

7 a These five words from Text 7B are difficult to spell.

occasionally   privilege   acknowledge   extraordinary   restaurant

   i Study the words and think of a mnemonic (which may be a rule, acronym or rhyme) for remembering how to spell each of them.
   ii Give your partner a spelling test, jumbling the order of the words.
   iii Mark each other's test and study closely any you got wrong.

b Look at the position of the word *only* in this sentence from the passage.

In Bulgaria the last tortoise restaurant closed only in the 1980s.

Copy and complete the sentences below to show their differences of meaning.

   i Only I saw a tortoise . . .
   ii I only saw a tortoise . . .
   iii I saw only a tortoise . . .

What is the rule for the positioning of the word *only* in a sentence?

c Why does the third paragraph begin with a question addressed to the reader? Do you think it is for the same reason as in Text 7A? Read the key point to help you decide.

Key point

Rhetorical questions

Rhetorical questions are a device mainly used in argument for the purpose of persuasion. They cannot be answered because the person to whom the question is addressed is not present, or is present but has no answer, and the speaker does not wait for one. However, rhetorical questions can also be used in narrative and descriptive writing if the writer wants to engage and involve the reader through suspense or empathy.

8 **a** Label the four stages of the seasonal cycle of the tree in the photographs.

b Describe, in a few sentences for each picture, the different appearances of the tree, the sky and the ground below.

c Write a sentence to explain why you think trees are often used as a symbol of time.

The banyan tree

O you shaggy-headed banyan tree standing on the bank of the pond, have you forgotten the little child, like the birds that have nested in your branches and left you?

Do you not remember how he sat at the window and wondered at the tangle of your roots that plunged underground?

The women would come to fill their jars in the pond, and your huge black shadow would wriggle on the water like sleep struggling to wake up.

Sunlight danced on the ripples like restless tiny shuttles weaving golden tapestry.

Two ducks swam by the weedy margin above their shadows, and the child would sit still and think.

He longed to be the wind and blow through your rustling branches, to be your shadow and lengthen with the day on the water, to be a bird and perch on your top-most twig, and to float like those ducks among the weeds and shadows.

Rabindranath Tagore

9 Discuss these questions with a partner and then tell the class what you think.

a Why do you think the poet addresses the tree and asks it questions in Text 7C?

b Which images do you find effective, and why?

c What do you think the poem is saying about the theme of time?

Text 7D

Friend

Do you remember
that wild stretch of land
with the lone tree guarding the point
from the sharp-tongued sea?

The fort we built out of branches
wrenched from the tree is dead wood now.
The air that was thick with the whirr of
toetoe spears succumbs at last to the grey gull's wheel.

Oyster-studded roots
of the mangrove yield no finer feast
of silver-bellied eels, and sea-snails
cooked in a rusty can.

Allow me to mend the broken ends
of shared days:
but I wanted to say
that the tree we climbed
that gave food and drink
to youthful dreams, is no more.
Pursed to the lips her fine-edged
leaves made whistle – now stamp
no silken **tracery** on the cracked
clay floor.

Friend,
in this drear
dreamless time I clasp
your hand if only for reassurance
that all our jewelled fantasies were
real and wore splendid rags.

Perhaps the tree
will strike fresh roots again:
give soothing shade to a hurt and
troubled world.

Hone Tuwhare

| **toetoe** | tall reed-like grass |
| **tracery** | elaborate pattern |

10 **a** Put into your own words the following phrases from Text 7D:
- the sharp-tongued sea
- the grey gull's wheel
- gave food and drink to youthful dreams

b Why do you think the third verse is in italics?

c What is the poet saying to his friend?

11 Poem 7C is set in Bengal, India, early in the 20th century; Poem 7D is by a Maori poet and is set in New Zealand in the late 20th century. Work in pairs to compare the following features, and then present your ideas to the class:

a the sense of place

b the sense of time

c the layout and line length

d the messages of the poems

e the way the reader is made to feel

Give your own preference between the two poems, and reasons for it.

Key point

Comparing texts

The clearest structure to use when comparing two texts is as follows:
- Say in what ways the poems are similar, giving examples and quotations to support your views.
- Say in what ways the poems are different, giving examples and quotations to support your views.
- Say which one you prefer, and think is more effective, giving reasons for your judgement.

12 Working with a partner, study the timetable in Text 7E to find the following information.

a **i** Which bus route (and in which direction) stops earliest in the evening?

ii Which bus route has the longest interval between buses?

b **i** Which bus would you take to get to the football stadium from Pudong International Airport?

ii How much would it cost to go from the Galaxy hotel to the Longyang Road Metro station?

c Set your own three questions about information contained in the
bus timetable and swap with another pair. Mark their answers when
they return them to you.

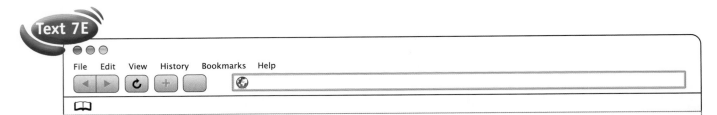

Shanghai bus timetable

NB fares quoted in Renminbi (RMB)

Route: Airport bus Line No. 1
From Pudong International Airport to
Hongqiao International Airport,
operating hours 7:20–23:00
From Hongqiao International
Airport to Pudong International Airport,
operating hours 6:00–21:00
Interval (mins): 10
Fare (RMB): 30
Stops: none

Route: Airport bus Line No. 3
From Pudong International Airport to
Galaxy hotel,
operating hours 7:00–23:00
From Galaxy hotel to Pudong
International Airport,
operating hours 5:30–20:00
Interval (mins): 15–20
Fare (RMB): 20
Stops: Xu Jiahui, Da Puqiao, Longyang Rd
Metro station

Route: Airport bus Line No. 2
From Pudong International Airport to
City Air Terminal,
operating hours 7:20–23:00
From City Air Terminal (Jingan temple) to
Pudong International Airport,
operating hours 6:00–21:30
Interval (mins): 10
Fare (RMB): 19
Stops: none

Route: Airport bus Line No. 4
From Pudong International Airport to
Hongkou football stadium,
operating hours 7:20–23:00
From Hongkou football stadium to
Pudong International Airport,
operating hours 5:40–21:00
Interval (mins): 15
Fare (RMB): 18
Stops: Deping Rd, Wu Jiaochang,
Da Baishu, East Jiangwan Rd

Route: Airport bus Line No. 5
From Pudong International Airport to
Shanghai Railway Station,
operating hours 7:20–23:00
From Shanghai Railway Station to
Pudong International Airport,
operating hours 5:30–21:00
Interval (mins): 15
Fare (RMB): 18
Stops: Pudong Avenue, Oriental hospital,
Middle Yan An Rd

Route: Airport bus Line No. 6
From Pudong International Airport to
Zhongshan Park,
operating hours 7:35–23:00
From Zhongshan Park to Pudong
International Airport,
operating hours 7:35–23:00
Interval (mins): 20–30
Fare (RMB): 20
Stops: Zhangjiang HighTech Park,
Longyang Rd, Dongfang Rd, Laoximen,
Shimen Rd, Huashan Rd

Text 7F on the next page is a poem about Ozymandias, the Greek name for the
Ancient Egyptian pharaoh Rameses II.

 a Draw a picture of the scene described in Text 7F, including as much
detail as possible.

b In one sentence of your own words, describe the character of
Ozymandias, as inferred from the poem.

c In one sentence of your own words, give the message of the poem. Think
about irony.

Text 7F

Ozymandias

I met a traveller from an antique land
Who said: Two vast and trunkless legs of stone
Stand in the desert . . . near them, on the sand,
Half sunk, a shattered visage lies, whose frown,
And wrinkled lip, and sneer of cold command,
Tell that its sculptor well those passions read
Which yet survive, stamped on these lifeless things,
The hand that mocked them, and the heart that fed.
And on the pedestal these words appear:
'My name is Ozymandias, king of kings:
Look on my works, ye Mighty, and despair!'
Nothing beside remains. Round the decay
Of that colossal wreck, boundless and bare
The lone and level sands stretch far away.

P.B. Shelley

14 Discuss and decide with a partner the effect of:

a the existence of three personae in the poem

b the use of direct speech and quotation in the poem

c the last line of the poem.

15 The poem in Text 7F is in a form that has a special name; it is called a sonnet.

a Count the number of lines in the poem, and look at the way they are grouped.

b Look at the rhyme scheme and the metre of the poem.

c Write a definition of a sonnet based on your answers to parts a and b.

Key point

Sonnets

Sonnets were a popular form of poetry in Shakespeare's time – he himself wrote 154 of them – and poets have produced sonnets ever since, although they are now often less strict in observing the original features of the genre.

Time has always been a popular theme (idea for exploration) in sonnets. Many of Shakespeare's sonnets examine the effects of the passing of time on nature and on humans, especially beautiful women. Shelley is doing something similar in 'Ozymandias'.

One of the main characteristics of a sonnet (defined as 14 lines of rhymed iambic pentameter) is that the final two lines (usually a rhymed pair, i.e. a couplet) arrive at a conclusion and give an answer to the question on which the poem is based.

Text 7G on the next page is a speech from Shakespeare's play *As You Like It*. It is known as 'the seven ages of man'.

 a Using a copy of Text 7G, mark off the different stages of human life. List the seven stages according to the extract.

b Explain in your own words the metaphor in the first four and a half lines of the extract.

c Write a list, numbered 1 to 7, of what happens in each of the stages of human life, according to the extract. Summarise each stage in one sentence of your own words.

 a Summarise in one sentence what you think the extract is saying about human existence. Does the rest of the class agree with your interpretation? Discuss whether Shakespeare's character is giving a fair picture of the human timeline.

b Do you think this description still applies today? Write notes for a list of the seven modern stages of the human life cycle.

c Read the tip on the next page and write your own version of the seven ages of man. You can then illustrate it to display in your classroom.

Text 7G

[. . .] All the world's a stage,
And all the men and women merely players:
They have their exits and their entrances
And one man in his time plays many parts,
His acts being seven ages. At first the infant,
Mewling and puking in the nurse's arms;
Then, the whining schoolboy with his satchel
And shining morning face, creeping like snail
Unwillingly to school; and then the lover,
Sighing like furnace, with a woeful ballad
Made to his mistress' eyebrow; then a soldier,
Full of strange oaths and bearded like the **pard**,
Jealous in honour, sudden, and quick in quarrel,
Seeking the bubble 'reputation'
Even in the cannon's mouth; and then the **justice**,
In fair round belly with good **capon** lined,
With eyes severe and beard of formal cut,
Full of wise **saws** and modern **instances** –
And so he plays his part; the sixth age shifts
Into the lean and slippered **pantaloon**,
With spectacles on nose and pouch on side,
His youthful **hose** well saved – a world too wide
For his shrunk **shank**; and his big manly voice,
Turning again toward childish **treble**, pipes
And whistles in his sound; last scene of all
That ends this strange eventful history
Is second childishness and mere oblivion,
Sans teeth, sans eyes, sans taste, sans everything.

pard	leopard	**instances**	examples	**treble**	high-pitched voice
justice	judge	**pantaloon**	aged buffoon	**sans**	without
capon	chicken	**hose**	trousers		
saws	sayings	**shank**	lower leg		

 Tip

For Activity 17c
The seven ages of man

Your version of the seven ages of man does not have to be in iambic pentameter, or any kind of verse, but can be in prose or as a numbered list. This extract comes from one of Shakespeare's comedy plays. Try to make your version humorous. You can do this by choosing amusing images, by making the physical appearances grotesque, and by exaggerating for effect.

UNIT 8 Exotic places

In this unit you will learn about creating exotic and powerful atmospheres and describing processes and objects in fiction and non-fiction. You will look at characterisation and setting devices in fictional prose, as well as further punctuation, vocabulary, sentence formation and grammar structures.

Activities

1

a What places do you think of as being far away, off the tourist routes and where people rarely visit?

b Where would you choose to go, and why, if you could go to a remote place?

c Do you think global travel and communications are having a beneficial effect on places or not? Give reasons for your answer.

Here is a selection of extracts describing the Sahara at night, taken from the memoir of a French pilot who crashed and was stranded in the desert in 1935.

Text 8A

i   The first stars tremble as if **shimmering** in green water. It will be a long time yet before they harden into diamonds. And still longer before I can **witness** the silent games of the shooting stars. Deep in the heart of some nights, I have seen so many racing sparks that it seemed as if a great wind were blowing among the stars.

ii Gathered for the night on our village square, that patch of sand lit by the flickering light from our crates, we waited. We were waiting for the dawn that would save us. And something **indefinable** gave that night the flavour of Christmas. We shared memories, we bantered and we sang. We tasted the gentle excitement of a well planned celebration. And yet we were **infinitely destitute**. Wind, sand and stars. **Austere** even for a **Trappist**. But on that poorly lit patch, six or seven men who possessed nothing in the world but their memories were sharing invisible riches.

> **iii** The golden hills offered up their **luminous** slopes to the moon, and others rose up in the shadow to its **frontier** with the light. In this deserted factory of darkness and moonlight there **reigned** the peace of work in abeyance and the silence of a trap, and I fell asleep within it.
>
> When I awoke I saw nothing but the pool of the night sky, for I was lying on a ridge with my arms stretched out, facing that hatchery of stars. With no understanding at that moment of those depths, I was seized by **vertigo**, for with no root to cling to, no roof or tree branch between those depths and me, I was already adrift and sinking, abandoned to my fall like a diver.
>
> *From* Wind, Sand and Stars *by Antoine de Saint-Exupéry*

| Trappist | a monk or nun |

2 a Listen to the three extracts being read aloud. Decide which one you think is most evocative of the atmosphere of night-time in the desert. Share your opinion and reasons with the class.

b Summarise in no more than three sentences, taking points from each of the three extracts, what the pilot is saying about the desert at night. Remember to use your own words and avoid repetition and irrelevance.

c Choose the correct answer to each of the following, one for each of the extracts. Write the complete sentences in your notebook.
  i The author thinks that the stars are like water / jewels / fire / wind.
  ii The author is waiting for rescue / a feast / monks / daylight.
  iii The author sees a trap / sand dunes / a factory / a pool.

3 Work with a partner on these vocabulary and grammar activities.

a Give synonyms which could exactly replace the ten words in bold in Text 8A.
  i   shimmering   iv infinitely   vii luminous   ix reigned
  ii witness   v destitute   viii frontier   x vertigo
  iii indefinable   vi austere

b Notice that the second extract is not entirely written in sentences. Rewrite it after the first sentence, using connectives and inserting words to form complex sentences.

c Passages ii and iii contain the expression 'nothing . . . but'. What is the effect of this usage?

Text 8B is an extract from *The Jungle Book*. It tells of the boy, Mowgli, being found and what happens at the Council of the Wolves (the wolves call themselves Free People).

Text 8B

The bushes rustled a little in the thicket, and Father Wolf dropped with his haunches under him, ready for his leap. He made his bound before he saw what it was he was jumping at, and then he tried to stop himself. The result was that he shot up straight into the air for four or five feet, landing almost where he left ground.

'Man!' he snapped. 'A man's cub. Look!'

Directly in front of him, holding on by a low branch, stood a naked brown baby who could just walk. He looked up into Father Wolf's face, and laughed.

'Is that a man's cub?' said Mother Wolf. 'I have never seen one. Bring it here.'

A Wolf accustomed to moving his own cubs can, if necessary, mouth an egg without breaking it, and though Father Wolf's jaws closed right on the child's back not a tooth even scratched the skin as he laid it down among the cubs.

'How little! How naked, and – how bold!' said Mother Wolf softly. The baby was pushing his way between the cubs to get close to the warm hide. 'Now, was there ever a wolf that could boast of a man's cub among her children?'

'I have heard now and again of such a thing, but never in our Pack or in my time,' said Father Wolf. 'He is altogether without hair, and I could kill him with a touch of my foot. But see, he looks up and is not afraid.'

The moonlight was blocked out of the mouth of the cave, for Shere Khan's great square head and shoulders were thrust into the entrance.

*   *   *   *

'Shere Khan does us great honour,' said Father Wolf, but his eyes were very angry. 'What does Shere Khan need?'

'My quarry. A man's cub went this way,' said Shere Khan. 'Its parents have run off. Give it to me.'

But Father Wolf knew that the mouth of the cave was too narrow for a tiger to come in by. Even where he was, Shere Khan's shoulders and forepaws were cramped for want of room.

'The Wolves are a free people,' said Father Wolf. 'They take orders from the Head of the Pack, and not from any striped cattle-killer. The man's cub is ours – to kill if we choose.'

'Ye choose and ye do not choose! What talk is this of choosing? It is I, Shere Khan, who speak!'

The tiger's roar filled the cave with thunder. Mother Wolf shook herself clear of the cubs and sprang forward, her eyes, like two green moons in the darkness, facing the blazing eyes of Shere Khan.

'And it is I, Raksha The Demon, who answers. The man's cub is mine, Lungri – mine to me! He shall not be killed. He shall live to run with the Pack and to hunt with the Pack; and in the end, look you, hunter of little naked cubs-frog-eater-fish-killer – he shall hunt thee!

Father Wolf looked on amazed. He had almost forgotten the days when he won Mother Wolf in fair fight from five other wolves, when she ran in the Pack and was not called The Demon for compliment's sake. Shere Khan might have faced Father Wolf, but he could not stand up against Mother Wolf, for he knew that where he was she had all the advantage of the ground, and would fight to the death. So he backed out of the cave mouth growling, and when he was clear he shouted:

'Each dog barks in his own yard! We will see what the Pack will say to this fostering of man-cubs. The cub is mine, and to my teeth he will come in the end, O bush-tailed thieves!'

Mother Wolf threw herself down panting among the cubs, and Father Wolf said to her gravely:

'Shere Khan speaks this much truth. The cub must be shown to the Pack. Wilt thou still keep him, Mother?'

'Keep him!' she gasped. 'He came naked, by night, alone and very hungry; yet he was not afraid! And that lame butcher would have killed him and would have run off to the Waingunga while the villagers here hunted through all our lairs in revenge! Keep him? Assuredly I will keep him. Lie still, little frog. O thou Mowgli – for Mowgli the Frog I will call thee – the time will come when thou wilt hunt Shere Khan as he has hunted thee.'

'But what will our Pack say?' said Father Wolf.

*　　*　　*　　*

Father Wolf waited till his cubs could run a little, and then on the night of the Pack Meeting took them and Mowgli and Mother Wolf to the Council Rock – a hilltop covered with stones and boulders where a hundred wolves could hide. Akela, the great gray Lone Wolf, who led all the Pack by strength and cunning, lay out at full length on his rock, and below him sat forty or more wolves of every size and colour. The Lone Wolf had led them for a year now. He had fallen twice into a wolf trap in his youth, and once he had been beaten and left for dead; so he knew the manners and customs of men. There was very little talking at the Rock. Akela from his rock would cry: 'Ye know the Law – ye know the Law. Look well, O Wolves!'

At last Father Wolf pushed 'Mowgli the Frog' into the centre, where he sat laughing and playing with some pebbles that glistened in the moonlight.

Akela never raised his head from his paws. A muffled roar came up from behind the rocks – the voice of Shere Khan crying: 'The cub is mine. Give him to me. What have the Free People to do with a man's cub?' Akela never even twitched his ears. All he said was: 'Look well, O Wolves!'

There was a chorus of deep growls, and a young wolf in his fourth year flung back Shere Khan's question to Akela: 'What have the Free People to do with a man's cub?' Now, the Law of the Jungle lays down that if there is any dispute as to the right of a cub to be accepted by the Pack, he must be spoken for by at least two members of the Pack who are not his father and mother.

'Who speaks for this cub?' said Akela. 'Among the Free People who speaks?' There was no answer and Mother Wolf got ready for what she knew would be her last fight, if things came to fighting.

Then the only other creature who is allowed at the Pack Council – Baloo, the sleepy brown bear who teaches the wolf cubs the Law of the Jungle: old Baloo, who can come and go where he pleases because he eats only nuts and roots and honey – rose upon his hind quarters and grunted.

'I speak for the man's cub. There is no harm in a man's cub. I have no gift of words, but I speak the truth. Let him run with the Pack, and be entered with the others. I myself will teach him.'

'We need yet another,' said Akela. 'Baloo has spoken, and he is our teacher for the young cubs. Who speaks besides Baloo?'

A black shadow dropped down into the circle. It was Bagheera the Black Panther, inky black all over, but with the panther

markings showing up in certain lights like the pattern of watered silk. Everybody knew Bagheera, and nobody cared to cross his path; for he was as cunning as the jackal, as bold as the wild buffalo, and as reckless as the wounded elephant. But he had a voice as soft as wild honey dripping from a tree, and a skin softer than down.

'O Akela, and ye the Free People,' he purred, 'I have no right in your assembly, but the Law of the Jungle says that if there is a doubt which is not a killing matter in regard to a new cub, the life of that cub may be bought at a price. And the Law does not say who may or may not pay that price. Am I right?'

'Good! Good!' said the young wolves, who are always hungry. 'Listen to Bagheera. The cub can be bought for a price. It is the Law.'

'To kill a naked cub is shame. Besides, he may make better sport for you when he is grown. Baloo has spoken in his behalf. Now to Baloo's word I will add one bull, and a fat one, newly killed, not half a mile from here, if ye will accept the man's cub according to the Law. Is it difficult?'

There was a clamour of scores of voices, saying: 'What matter? He will die in the winter rains. He will scorch in the sun. What harm can a naked frog do us? Let him run with the Pack. Where is the bull, Bagheera? Let him be accepted.' And then came Akela's deep bay, crying: 'Look well – look well, O Wolves!'

Mowgli was still deeply interested in the pebbles, and he did not notice when the wolves came and looked at him one by one. At last they all went down the hill for the dead bull, and only Akela, Bagheera, Baloo, and Mowgli's own wolves were left. Shere Khan roared still in the night, for he was very angry that Mowgli had not been handed over to him.

'Ay, roar well,' said Bagheera, under his whiskers, 'for the time will come when this naked thing will make thee roar to another tune, or I know nothing of man.'

'It was well done,' said Akela. 'Men and their cubs are very wise. He may be a help in time.'

'Truly, a help in time of need; for none can hope to lead the Pack forever,' said Bagheera.

Akela said nothing. He was thinking of the time that comes to every leader of every pack when his strength goes from him and he gets feebler and feebler, till at last he is killed by the wolves and a new leader comes up – to be killed in his turn.

'Take him away,' he said to Father Wolf, 'and train him as befits one of the Free People.'

And that is how Mowgli was entered into the Seeonee Wolf Pack for the price of a bull and on Baloo's good word.

From The Jungle Book *by Rudyard Kipling*

4 **a** Listen to or participate in the reading aloud of Text 8B with different voices for the six different speaking animals and another voice filling in the narration.

b Discuss how the use of content and language is intended to appeal to young readers.

c Find examples of old-fashioned forms of vocabulary, grammar or punctuation and discuss why they are used in the passage.

5 Working with a partner, answer these questions.

a Can you find five phrases from the first part of Text 8B which convey that Father Wolf:
  i carried the boy gently
  ii could easily kill the boy
  iii does not respect Shere Khan
  iv admires Mother Wolf's courage
  v is concerned about the boy's future?

b What arguments are being presented in the second part of the passage, and who is making them?

c Which words and phrases in the passage describe the appearance, behaviour and speech of the different animal types? Say in your own words what kind of character they represent.

Animal	Phrase	Character
wolf		
tiger		
bear		
panther		

6 Discuss the questions below in your class.

a The phrase 'Law of the Jungle' as used in Text 8B can have various possible interpretations. What does it mean to you?

b How do you think the passage prefigures what is to happen later in the book? What can you predict about future relationships and events, and what is your evidence?

c This passage appears to be about animals deciding what should happen to a baby boy found abandoned in the jungle. What other meanings can you find in the text?

The writer of Text 8C, New Zealander Helen Thayer, was the first woman to travel alone to the Magnetic North Pole. Her only companion was a husky dog called Charlie.

Meeting a polar bear

I put my day's supply of food into my day food bag and then began to pack the tent. I was completely engrossed in pulling the freezing tent poles out of the ice, when suddenly I heard a deep, long growl coming from the depths of Charlie's throat. I looked at him and then in the direction in which he was staring. Even before I looked I knew what I would see. A polar bear!

It was a female followed by two cubs coming slowly, purposefully, plodding through the rough shore ice towards me. They were 200 metres away. With a pounding heart I grabbed my loaded rifle and flare gun and carefully walked sideways a few steps to Charlie, who was snarling with a savagery that caught my breath. Without taking my eyes off the bear, I unclipped Charlie from his ice anchor and, again walking sideways, I led him to the sled where I clipped his chain to a tie-down rope.

The bear, now only 150 metres away, wasn't stopping. Her cubs had dropped back but she came on with a steady measured stride, while I frantically tried to remember all the advice I had been given. Keep eye contact, move sideways or slightly forward, never backward, stay calm, don't show fear, stand beside a tent, sled, or other large object to make my short body appear as large as possible. Don't shoot unless forced to. Don't wound a bear – you'll make it even more dangerous – and never run. Repeating to myself, 'Stay calm, stay calm,' I fired a warning shot to the bear's left. The loud explosion had no effect. On she came. I fired a flare, landing it a little to her right. Her head moved slightly in its direction but she didn't stop. I fired another flare, this time dropping it right in front of her. She stopped, looked at the flare burning a bright red on the white ice, then looked at me. She was only 30 metres away now.

By this time my nerves were as tight as violin strings and my heart could have been heard at base camp. The bear began to step around the flare, and I dropped another a metre in front of her. Again she stopped, looked at the flare and at me. Then she fixed her tiny black eyes on Charlie, who was straining at the end of his chain, snapping and snarling, trying to reach her. She looked back at her cubs. I could sense her concern about Charlie's snarling and her cubs. She waited for her cubs to catch up, then moved to my left in a half circle. I fired two more flares in quick succession, trying to draw a line between her and me. She stopped, then moved back towards my right. I fired two more flares and again she stopped. She seemed to want to cross the line of flares but was unsure of the result and of Charlie, so she elected to stay back. She kept moving right in a half circle, still 30 metres away. Finally, with a last long look she plodded north with her two new cubs trotting behind her, their snow-white coats contrasting with their mother's creamy, pale yellow colour.

The whole episode lasted 15 minutes but seemed years long. My hands were shaking as I stood, still holding my rifle and flare gun, watching the trio slowly move north. But in spite of the mind-numbing fear that still gripped me, I could feel deep down inside a real satisfaction. I now knew that I could stand up to a bear in the wild and stay calm enough to function. With Charlie's help I had passed my first test.

From Polar Dream *by Helen Thayer*

 7 This activity focuses on the punctuation and language of Text 8C.

a Rewrite the following extract from the passage, changing the punctuation to show:
- how colons and semi-colons are used to introduce and separate items in a list respectively
- different ways of indicating a parenthesis.

I frantically tried to remember all the advice I had been given. Keep eye contact, move sideways or slightly forward, never backward, stay calm, don't show fear, stand beside a tent, sled, or other large object to make your body appear as large as possible. Don't shoot unless forced to. Don't wound a bear – you'll make it even more dangerous – and never run.

b Explain how a change of position of the comma from before to after *still* in the quotation below would change its meaning.

> My hands were shaking as I stood, still holding my rifle and flare gun . . .

c Find examples in the passage of:
   i hyperbole (exaggeration for effect)   ii cliché.

8 a Write a list of tips, beginning with *Do* or *Don't*, for how to respond when approached by a polar bear, taking your facts from paragraphs two and three of Text 8C. Compare your list with a partner's.

b Look for redundancy (unnecessary or repeated material) in the passage. On a copy of Text 8C, put brackets around the parts of the passage (words, phrases and whole sentences) which could be removed without losing any of the facts of the incident. Read the tip first to help you.

Tip

For Activity 8b
Narrative duration

Sometimes an account of an incident relies on repetition of the same action to make the situation seem more tense than if reported more economically and at the speed at which it really happened. The firing of the flares could be reduced to one sentence and described as a repeated action. Writers have to consider duration (how long things last) when giving an account, i.e. whether to make the amount of time taken to read about an action reflect the amount of time it took for it to be performed, or to take more or less time, as this has an effect on the narrative pace and impact of the description. For instance, 'He packed his suitcase, called a taxi and left the house' is a speeded-up process, whereas describing in great detail someone falling downstairs would take longer than the performance of the action.

c Imagine that you are going to turn the non-fiction account in Text 8C into a short story. Write the opening paragraph of the story, in which you introduce the character and setting, using information from the passage, and create a suitable atmosphere for what is to follow. Read your story opening to the class and agree on the most appropriate and engaging.

Text 8D is a description of the process of yam planting in Eastern Nigeria from the novel *Things Fall Apart* by Chinua Achebe, set at the end of the 19th century.

Text 8D

After the Week of Peace every man and his family began to clear the bush to make new farms. The cut bush was left to dry and fire was then set to it. As the smoke rose into the sky kites appeared from different directions and hovered over the burning field in silent valediction. The rainy season was approaching when they would go away until the dry season returned.

Okonkwo spent the next few days preparing his seed-yams. He looked at each yam carefully to see whether it was good for sowing. Sometimes he decided that a yam was too big to be sown as one seed and he split it deftly along its length with his sharp knife. His eldest son, Nwoye, and Ikemefuna helped him by fetching the yams in long baskets from the barn and in counting the prepared seeds in groups of four hundred.

Sometimes Okonkwo gave them a few yams each to prepare. But he always found fault with their effort, and he said so with much threatening. Inwardly Okonkwo knew that the boys were still too young to understand fully the difficult art of preparing seed-yams. But he thought that one could not begin too early. Yam stood for manliness, and he who could feed his family on yams from one harvest to another was a very great man indeed. Okonkwo wanted his son to be a great farmer and a great man.

Some days later, when the land had been moistened by two or three heavy

rains, Okonkwo and his family went to the farm with baskets of seed-yams, their hoes and **machetes**, and the planting began. They made single mounds of earth in straight lines all over the field and sowed the yams in them.

Yam, the king of crops, was a very exacting king. For three or four moons it demanded hard work and constant attention from cockcrow till the chickens went back to roost. The young tendrils were protected from earth-heat with rings of sisal leaves. As the rains became heavier the women planted maize, melons and beans between the yam mounds. The yams were then staked, first with little sticks and later with tall and big tree branches. The women weeded the farm three times at definite periods in the life of the yams, neither early nor late.

And now the rains had really come, so heavy and persistent that even the village rain-maker no longer claimed to be able to intervene. He could not stop the rain now, just as he would not attempt to start it in the heart of the dry season, without serious danger to his own health. The personal dynamism required to counter the forces of these extremes of weather would be far too great for the human frame.

And so nature was not interfered with in the middle of the rainy season. Sometimes it poured down in such thick sheets of water that earth and sky seemed merged in one grey wetness. It was then uncertain whether the low rumbling of **Amadiora's** thunder came from above or below. At such times, in each of the countless thatch huts of Umuofia, children sat around their mother's cooking fire telling stories, or with their father in his *obi* warming themselves from a log fire, roasting and eating maize. It was a brief resting period between the exacting and ardous planting season and the equally exacting but light-hearted month of harvests.

machetes	broad, heavy knives used as tools or weapons
Amadiora	Igbo god of the sky
obi	hut

9 Work in a small group to answer the following questions about Text 8D.

a According to the passage, are the following statements true or false?
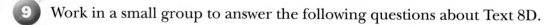
  i Kites go away for the dry season.
  ii Okonkwo was not impressed by the skills of the boys.
  iii Okonkwo believes one is never too young to start learning about yam planting.
  iv Men are judged by how good they are at growing yams.

v Yams should be planted in dry soil, before the rains come.
vi Yams need several months of hard work.
vii The women do the weeding of the yams.
viii The rain-maker tried in vain to stop the rain.
ix There were a few thatch huts in Umuofia.
x Harvesting is less demanding than planting.

b Explain the meaning of the following phrases from the passage in your own words:
- silent valediction
- a very exacting king
- personal dynamism.

c What is the effect of the use of simple sentences and simple and repeated vocabulary in the passage?

10 **a** There are places in the first three paragraphs of Text 8D where commas could be inserted or used to replace a full stop. On a copy of Text 8D, indicate where these places are. Give reasons for using the commas.

b List the stages of the yam growing process. Check with a partner to see if you have the same number and order of stages.

c There are many things to be learnt from the passage about life in an African village in the 19th century. List as many as you can, to do with relationships, living conditions, work, and expectations. Contribute to a class discussion of the ways in which it is different from your own life.

The sentences in Text 8E describe the life of reindeer herders in Siberia.

Way of life on thin ice

- The Chukchi have been herding their reindeer across the frozen wilderness of the Chukchi Peninsula in north-east Siberia for generations.
- Rising temperatures are shrinking the snow-covered landscape.
- Families are being forced to move to villages and towns in search of other work.

- Despite their thick coats of reindeer fur, the herders are still at the mercy of the bitter cold, returning to base with ice hanging from their faces after a day of herding reindeer.
- The temperatures go as low as –30°C.
- The herders line their boots with dried grass for insulation.
- They have to keep a lookout for grey and polar wolves.
- Predators pose a serious threat; the reindeer are watched over day and night, while any strays have to be recovered on foot.
- The herders cover upwards of 15 kilometres of ground each day.
- With resources scarce, families scratch a subsistence living. Meals consist of a small portion of reindeer meat and seal fat three or four times a day.
- They have to keep their energy levels up.

11 Your task is to write an article based on the facts in Text 8E.

   a Put numbers next to each of the sentences on a copy of Text 8E to form a logical sequence to the information.

   b Decide which numbered points to connect together to make complex sentences. Decide how many paragraphs you need.

   c Write the connected piece of writing to describe the lives of the reindeer herders, as though it comes from a magazine article.

12 Bring from home an unusual and exotic object which comes from a part of the world distant from where you live for example, a fan, an ornament, a hat.

   a Make notes about the object's history.
   - Did you or someone else bring it back from a trip abroad?
   - Where was it bought, and how much did it cost?
   - What does it tell you about its country of origin?
   - How long ago was it acquired, and where has it been since?
   - What memories are associated with it?

   b Study the object closely. Make notes on all its aspects, using as many descriptive details as you can. Think about size, shape, colour, texture, and evoke as many senses as possible.

   c Deliver a 'show and tell' to the rest of the class, using the ideas you have prepared but not reading from a script.

Text 8F is a short story extract. In the extract, Nicholas disobeys his aunt and visits the forbidden lumber-room in the attic, where he discovers an array of exotic things from faraway places.

Text 8F

The key turned stiffly in the lock, but it turned. The door opened, and Nicholas was in an unknown land.

Often and often Nicholas had pictured to himself what the lumber-room might be like, that region that was so carefully sealed from youthful eyes and concerning which no questions were ever answered. It came up to his expectations. In the first place it was large and dimly lit, one high window opening on to the forbidden garden being its only source of illumination. In the second place it was a storehouse of unimagined treasures. Such parts of the house as Nicholas knew best were rather bare and cheerless, but here there were wonderful things for the eye to feast on. First and foremost there was a piece of framed tapestry that was evidently meant to be a fire-screen. To Nicholas it was a living, breathing story; he sat down on a roll of Indian hangings, glowing in wonderful colours beneath a layer of dust, and took in all the details of the tapestry picture.

There were other objects of delight and interest claiming his instant attention: here were quaint twisted candlesticks in the shape of snakes, and a teapot fashioned like a china duck, out of whose open beak the tea was supposed to come. How dull and shapeless the nursery teapot seemed in comparison! And there was a carved sandal-wood box packed tight with aromatic cotton-wool, and between the layers of cotton-wool were little brass figures, hump-necked bulls, and peacocks and goblins, delightful to see and to handle. Less promising in appearance was a large

> square book with plain black covers; Nicholas peeped into it, and, behold, it was full of coloured pictures of birds. And such birds! In the garden, and in the lanes when he went for a walk, Nicholas came across a few birds, of which the largest were an occasional magpie or wood-pigeon; here were herons and bustards, kites, toucans, tiger-bitterns, brush turkeys, ibises, golden pheasants, a whole portrait gallery of undreamed-of creatures. And as he was admiring the colouring of the mandarin duck and assigning a life-history to it, the voice of his aunt in shrill vociferation of his name came from the gooseberry garden without.
>
> *From 'The Lumber-Room' by Saki*

13 In this activity you will consider the effect on the reader of Text 8F.

   a What impression do you get of the character of Nicholas from Text 8F? Give reasons.

   b What impression do you get of the character of his aunt from the comments about her and her house in the passage?

   c Where is the reader's sympathy in the passage, and how has this been achieved?

14 **a** On a copy of Text 8F, circle the following and explain how they are being used:
     i colons (:) and semi-colons (;)
     ii hyphens
     iii 'And' to begin a sentence.

   b What was it that so fascinated Nicholas about the objects in the lumber-room in Text 8F? Write a sentence to summarise his interest in them.

   c How do the style and the content of the passage convey the delight of Nicholas in the lumber-room? Note the devices used to make the tone seem enthusiastic.

15 Plan and write your own descriptive piece, of about a page, beginning, 'It was a storehouse of unimagined treasures.' First read the key point and tip on the next page to help you.

Key point

Time frame for descriptive writing

There is a danger in writing description that it will seem dull because it is static. Although a descriptive writing task is different from a narrative, which has characters and events, it is acceptable to describe the place or action changing during a short time period (as for a description of a thunderstorm or sunset, for instance). This gives the writer more stages to describe, a process to record, and therefore gives an opportunity for a wider range of descriptive language to be used. Alternatively, it can be the observer rather than the observed which moves and brings change into the descriptive process; either of these techniques make the piece more interesting and engaging for the reader.

For Activity 15
Description of objects

Describe in your response what your persona – which may be first or third person – sees as they turn around in a room in which strange objects have been hidden away. Think about colours, shapes and textures, as well as the senses of sight and smell. To create an atmosphere of the fascinatingly exotic, everything needs to seem unusual, out of this world, to the observer, wherever they happen to be. Be careful that your piece doesn't become simply a list; you need to describe each object fully before moving on to the next. There need be no connection between the objects, as a junk store contains a random assortment of things which find themselves together by chance. It is a good idea to try to create some contrasts and to include objects that one might not expect to find there to give an element of surprise and added interest.

UNIT 9 Travel and transport

This unit focuses on place description in travel writing, advertising and fiction, looking at how descriptive language is used differently according to purpose. You will have the opportunity to try out these different kinds of writing yourself.

Activities

1

a Make a list of places that you have travelled to, and give them a mark out of ten for how much you enjoyed them. Be prepared to give reasons to the class for your evaluations.

b Make a 'wish list' of five places you have always wanted to visit, and next to each place give a reason for feeling attracted to go there. Compare with a partner to see whether you have chosen any of the same places.

c Working with a partner, copy the table below into your notebook and complete it by adding the advantages and disadvantages of the ten forms of transport.

Means of transport	Advantages	Disadvantages
car		
train		
bus		
plane		
ship		
horse		
motorbike		
bicycle		
hot air balloon		
on foot		

The extracts in Text 9A on the next page are from a book describing travel in Spain. Some words have been removed.

Text 9A

i Now it was the end of September and I'd reached the sea, having taken almost three months to come down through Spain. Cádiz, from a distance, was a city of sharp ____ , a ____ of white on a ____ of blue ____ , lying curved on the bay like a ____ and sparkling with African light.

ii The Galician night came quickly, the hills turned ____ and the valleys flooded with ____ shadow. The ____ coastline below, now dark and glittering, looked like sweepings of broken glass. Vigo was cold and ____ , an unlighted ruin, already smothered in the ____ blue dusk. Only the sky and the ocean stayed alive, running with ____ streams of flame. Then as the sun went down it seemed to drag the whole sky with it like the shreds of a ____ curtain, leaving rags of bright water that went on smoking and smouldering along the estuaries and around the many islands.

iii Segovia was a city in a valley of stones – a compact, half-forgotten heap of architectural splendours built for the glory of some other time. Here were churches, castles, and medieval walls standing sharp in the evening light, but all [1] ____ by that extraordinary phenomenon of masonry, the Roman aqueduct, which [2] ____ the whole. It came [3] ____ from the hills in a series of arches, some rising to over 30 metres,

and composed of blocks of granite weighing several tons and held together by their weight alone. This imperial gesture, built to carry water from a spring 16 kilometres away, still [4] _____ across the valley with massive grace, a hundred vistas framed by its soaring arches, to enter the city at last high above the rooftops, [5] _____ like a mammoth among the houses.

From As I Walked Out One Midsummer Morning *by Laurie Lee*

2 On a copy of Text 9A, fill in the gaps in the three descriptions of Spanish towns. Work with a partner.

   a Put the five nouns below in the correct gaps in extract i.

     sheet   scribble   scimitar   glass   incandescence

   b Choose the best word from each line of adjectives to fill the seven gaps in extract ii.

grey	purple	black
heavy	thick	liquid
twisted	curved	jagged
dark	dim	gloomy
bright	unhealthy	dead
huge	immense	long
burning	smoking	flaming

   c Choose your own verbs to fill the five gaps in extract iii.

3 After your teacher has given you the correct answers for Activities 2a and 2b, contribute to a class discussion.

   a Discuss why the writer chose those words in extract i, considering the effect of each word in that particular place.

   b Consider the effect of the writer's chosen words in extract ii and why they are better than the other words in the lists.

   c Tell the class which words you put into the gaps in Activity 2c, and justify your choices. After your teacher has given you the correct answers, you may wish to argue that your choices are better than those used by the writer.

4 **a** Think of a town you have visited which has striking features of some kind, e.g. its location, architecture, buildings or public parks.

b Write down some adjectives and verbs which would best describe the position or features of the town, and then try to link some of them by using a sustained image.

c Draft and edit a half-page description of the town. Read it to the class or give it to your teacher.

For Activity 3
Travel writing

Travel writing is highly descriptive. Its aim is to evoke a strong sense of place and atmosphere. Although it is in prose, poetic devices are often used and words are chosen for their sensuous effect, predominantly the senses of sight and sound. A piece of effective descriptive writing must contain vocabulary and images which are appropriate and precise, but rhythm is also taken into account; the number of syllables may determine the choice of a word. Other aspects of sound may also be considered; assonance and alliteration may be employed to make words fit memorably together. Notice that in extract ii there is a sustained image, composed of *shreds*, *curtain* and *rags* which all continue the comparison of the sunset with a piece of material which is disintegrating because of being on fire.

Next you will look at examples of advertisements for holiday destinations.

5 Work with a partner to analyse the advertising language of Text 9B.

a List the present participle adjectives used in Text 9B and comment on the effect of this form of adjective.

b Identify imperative (command) verbs in the passage and comment on the effect of this verb form.

c Find six examples of intensifying adverbs (used to emphasise another word, e.g. 'very') in the passage and comment on their usage. Read the key point on page 134.

d Find examples of extreme or superlative words and phrases in the passage, and comment on their effect.

e Look at the lists in the passage. Why do you think they are there?

The Great Karoo

For a truly breathtaking South African adventure, come and explore the Great Karoo. The Great Karoo is an awe-inspiring landscape of undulating plains and soaring mountains, with some of the most spectacular scenery and wildlife to be found on earth. This unspoilt region still bears many traces of its ancient past, including rock paintings left by the hunters and shepherds who lived here many thousands of years ago. The places where you find it are very secluded, so the art is undamaged and totally magnificent.

The towns of the Great Karoo have their own welcoming atmosphere. There's a timelessness that is completely different from the big cities. This is perhaps the only place in South Africa where you still have real village life. Working farms with appealing guesthouses are some of the best places to stay here. See the traditional Karoo architectural style of walls of brick and stone, reed ceilings, poplar-wood roof timbers and a corrugated-iron roof.

The Great Karoo is a beckoning place of limitless adventures, where you can visit game reserves, or go horse-riding, hang-gliding or whitewater tubing. The dazzling scenery is just incredible; there's a never-ending display of wildlife: antelopes, wildebeest, jackals, wildcats, and the birdlife is really amazing.

So if you want a genuine thrill – and a fantastic holiday – don't delay: the Great Karoo is waiting for you.

6 Now consider the content and style of Text 9B.

a List the topics mentioned in Text 9B (e.g. wildlife).

b List the clichés used in the passage (e.g. 'unspoilt region').

c Write a paragraph describing a rural location, in the same style as the passage.

Text 9C

Spice up your life!

There are so many adventures waiting on the **magical** island of Grenada, the Spice of the Caribbean. If your idea of paradise involves white sands, swaying palms and balmy blue ocean, the Caribbean island of Grenada is your dream come true. This sun-kissed isle is truly **exotic, perfumed** with the spices for which it is famous, and boasting rainforests, mountains, waterfalls and lakes. And while it feels remote, it's easy to get to.

Whether you're taking a **romantic** break, travelling with friends or bringing the whole family, Grenada has endless attractions. There are more than 40 unspoilt white-sand shores to enjoy, such as Grand Anse Beach, a two-mile expanse curving around a peaceful bay. Fancy some adventure? There's so much to choose from: walking in Grand Etang National Park; going back in time to an **authentic** working 17th-century plantation; participating in a variety of water sports including snorkelling among the turtles; becoming an 18th-century pirate for the day on a replica pirate ship.

The island's capital, St George's, is widely regarded as one of the prettiest towns in the Caribbean, and its harbour is a great place to enjoy freshly caught seafood. The island abounds with **fragrant** spice trees, so there's no shortage of tasty Caribbean cuisine to enjoy. There are cocoa trees all over Grenada, and the beans are **harvested** to make **delicious** chocolate.

The island is full of superb resorts and **luxurious** hotels. Whatever you do on this **idyllic** Caribbean island, it is likely to be **pretty special**.

Cambridge Checkpoint English 8

7　a　On a copy of Text 9C, underline the features described which you recognise as typical of tropical islands.

　　b　Write down the connotations and associations of each of the ten adjectives in bold in the passage.

i	magical	v	authentic	ix	luxurious
ii	exotic	vi	fragrant	x	idyllic
iii	perfumed	vii	harvested		
iv	romantic	viii	delicious		

　　c　Summarise in one sentence what the advertisement is claiming about the island of Grenada.

8　Focus on the style and purpose of holiday advertisements, referring to Text 9C.

　　a　What are the colours used in holiday advertising, and why?

　　b　Identify the recurring word in Text 9C and say why you think it is repeated.

　　c　Why do you think sentences begin with *And*, *So* and *Or* in this type of writing?

9　Your task now is to write your own holiday advertisement.

　　a　Think of a name and location for an imaginary island.

　　b　Read the key point below, then make a list of the features of your island. In an adjacent column, list suitable phrases with which to describe them.

　　c　Using your lists, your notes for Activity 5, and Texts 9B and 9C as style models, write a one-page magazine advertisement for the island and give it to your teacher.

Key point

Advertising language

- Advertisements use recurring metaphors and puns, as in 'Spice up your life!'
- Positive colours are referred to, those which are associated with pleasure and relaxation, such as gold, blue, white and chocolate.
- Familiar not original ideas and language are the aim, so one can expect to find clichés like swaying palms and paradise, and dreams coming true.

- Alliteration is used to make the message stronger (e.g. *balmy blue*).
- Archaic vocabulary is employed to give a romantic, old-world feeling to a place (e.g. *isle*, *shores*).
- Hyphenated compound adjectives give a sense of abundance and richness, and introduce metaphors (e.g. *sun-kissed*).
- For a complete atmospheric effect, adverts for places include all five senses.
- Rhetorical questions are used to make it seem that the advertiser knows exactly what the reader desires, and that the need can be satisfied.
- Non-sentences, simple sentences or sentences beginning with *And*, *So* and *Or* are used to convey the idea of endless opportunities for enjoyment.

Text 9D is a list of facts and claims about a 15-day journey on Indian railways.

India's 'Palace on Wheels'

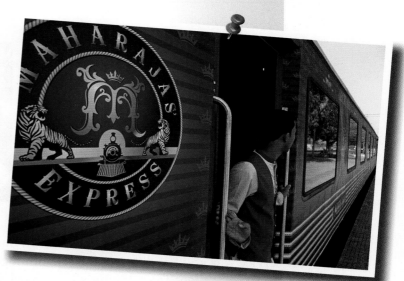

- It goes from the flat low ground to high mountainous areas.
- The start of the journey is in Delhi, which has the Red Fort.
- Accommodation is in five-star hotels.
- The hill-top city of Shimla can be visited by jeep and on foot.
- Shimla has a mixture of eastern and western architecture.
- This is the way the Maharajas travelled.
- The train stops at Jaipur, known as the Pink City, which has markets.
- In Jaipur there is the Palace of the Winds and the Amber Fort.
- There are tigers and leopards in the Ranthambore National Park.
- A camel ride through the sand dunes around Jaisalmer is scheduled.
- A cruise on Lake Pichola, around the small island, is included.
- The last leg of the trip is to the Agra Fort, built of red sandstone, and the Taj Mahal.

10 You are going to write a leaflet promoting the Indian railway journey described in Text 9D.

   a Decide how many paragraphs you will use, which facts you will put in each paragraph, and how you will link them.

   b Decide which verbs, adjectives and adverbs you will use, avoiding repetition.

   c Write your promotional leaflet of about one page with the title 'Tour India like a Prince!'.

The following are web reviews of hotels in Harare (Zimbabwe), Mexico City and New Delhi (India).

Text 9E

File   Edit   View   History   Bookmarks   Help

i Garden Hotel, Harare

I stayed at the Garden on a business trip, staying five nights in total. Upon arrival, the reception staff were very friendly. My room was comfortable; it was rather old-fashioned and hadn't been decorated for many a decade, but it contained the basic facilities, except for a fridge. The room was clean, the towels were plentiful and fresh, and there was a TV with English-speaking channels. There was sufficient choice at breakfast and eggs were cooked to order. On one occasion I ate dinner there too, and the service was good and the food tasty, although the menu is rather limited. The location is excellent for relaxing after a hard day's work. The beautiful gardens, with a variety of trees and plants, and animal sculptures amusingly positioned, are a hideaway in which you can sit outside in the day or at night in comfort and safety.

ii Hotel Casa del Halcón, Mexico City

We hadn't prebooked for our weekend stay, but were given a room at the front of the hotel overlooking the street and a lovely park with a fountain. It was quiet in the evening, owing to the area being more residential than commercial. Our room was cleaned daily. We had a hammock on our balcony and the bed was comfortable. A Mexican continental breakfast was included, and the kitchen staff were very obliging. The front desk staff were mostly very friendly and helpful, and probably would have been more so if we spoke Spanish. There are several good places to eat nearby, but they are not easy to find. The hotel is within walking distance of the metro station and bus stop. Breakfast was accompanied by loud recorded music we could have done without. The most important facility was the free WiFi.

iii   Royal Hotel, New Delhi

This is one of a chain of historic, high-standard hotels in India, all beautifully designed in perfect locations, but very different. I loved this one for its wonderful infinity pool, the great gym facilities, attentive staff and wonderful internal shopping area. The beds are so generously sized and comfortable that you will not want to get up in the morning. Because I was there for work, I ate alone each night at one of their many ethnic restaurants. The food each time was authentic and delicious. Don't miss the patisserie with its wonderful and unique cakes fashioned in the shapes of handbags or shoes.

11 a Which review in Text 9E do you find most persuasive and which hotel would you most like to stay in? Give your reasons.

  b List the aspects of the hotels that are mentioned in all three reviews.

  c Write a positive review, using the Text 9E examples as models, for a hotel you have stayed in or one you know, perhaps from a film. Read it to the class.

12 Text 9F on the next page is about a driverless car.

  a Write a sentence, in your own words as far as possible, to explain why the driverless car is safer than one with a driver, according to Text 9F.

  b Write a sentence, in your own words as far as possible, to explain how the car is able to drive safely.

  c Write a sentence to explain why you think the driverless car is a useful invention, giving reasons to support your view.

Text 9F

The Google Driverless Car

If there's anything more scary than a car with a mad or incompetent driver, it's a car with no driver, right? Not so, say the gurus of Google. A mixture of ultimate-tech mini-computers and the archived knowledge of Google's Streetview cameras mean that a driverless car is actually safer than one with a human being at the wheel.

And that's not just the view of a few techno-extremists at Google's Mountain View headquarters; as of May 2012, the state of Nevada in the USA has licensed Google's cars to drive on public highways with no human on board.

As long ago as 2005, the genius Sebastian Thrun, who works for Stanford University's Artificial Intelligence Laboratory, led a team which won a $2 million prize from the Department of Defense in the USA for developing an autonomous, driverless car. Since then, the concept has been refined to the point where the cautious lawmakers of Nevada believe that Google's car really can judge real-life road situations as well as, if not better than, a traditional driver.

How does it work? The car (a Toyota Prius, initially) is heavily modified with a stunning array of detectors, including radar, camera and LIDAR – a new technology using laser beams to map the area around the car with extraordinary precision and detail. The input of these sensors is integrated by a sophisticated Artificial Intelligence (AI) system, which compares the images with the stored Streetview database to work out exactly where the car is. The AI unit knows the layout of the road ahead and can drive efficiently to avoid sudden braking and acceleration. The sensors critically keep it aware of other traffic to avoid collisions.

And the final result? Nearly a quarter of a million kilometres driven on public roads without an accident. How many humans can claim such a record? And this is only the beginning.

13 **a** Think of another type of vehicle, and then imagine a revolutionary invention has been produced: for example, a skateboard which can be instructed what to do. Your table from Activity 1c may help you.

b Give your invention a name. List descriptive words and phrases to make your invention sound desirable.

c Using Text 9F as a model, write half a page to promote your invention and explain how it was developed.

Tip

For Activity 13
Describing an invention

You can make up any names, dates, places and claims you wish to give substance to the creation of your fictional vehicle. If they sound plausible your product will seem authentic and convince the reader that they should be interested in acquiring one. A catchy name is also part of the persuasive process; a battery-operated car launched in 1985 called the C5 did not catch on. The main thing to stress when trying to sell modes of transport is safety.

Text 9G is an extract from a novel set in Australia. It describes a landmark called Hanging Rock, to which a group of schoolgirls have gone on a picnic trip in 1900.

Text 9G

The creek had hardly been crossed before the Hanging Rock had risen up directly ahead of the four girls, clearly visible beyond a short grassy slope. The immediate impact of its soaring peaks induced a silence so impregnated with its powerful presence that even Edith was struck dumb. The splendid spectacle, as if by special arrangement between Heaven and the Head Mistress of Appleyard College, was brilliantly illuminated for their inspection. On the steep southern façade the play of golden light and deep violet shade revealed the intricate construction of long vertical slabs; some smooth as giant tombstones, others grooved and fluted by prehistoric architecture of wind and water, ice and fire. Huge boulders, originally spewed red hot from the boiling bowels of the earth, now come to rest, cooled and rounded in forest shade.

Confronted by such monumental configurations of nature the human eye is woefully inadequate. Who can say how many or how few of its unfolding marvels are actually seen, selected and recorded by the four pairs of eyes now fixed in staring wonder at the Hanging Rock? Does Marion Quade note the horizontal ledges crisscrossing the verticals of the main pattern whose geological formation must be memorised for next Monday's essay? Is Edith aware of

the hundreds of frail starlike flowers crushed under her tramping boots, while Irma catches the scarlet flash of a parrot's wing and thinks it a flame amongst the leaves? And Miranda, whose feet appear to be choosing their own way through the ferns as she tilts her head towards the glittering peaks, does she already feel herself more than a spectator agape at a holiday pantomime? So they walk silently towards the lower slopes, in single file, each locked in the private world of her own perceptions, unconscious of the strains and tensions of the molten mass that hold it anchored to the groaning earth: of the creakings and shudderings, the wandering airs and currents known only to the wise little bats, hanging upside down in its clammy caves. None of them see or hear the snake dragging its copper coils over the stones ahead. Nor the panic exodus of spiders, grubs and woodlice from rotting leaves and bark. There are no tracks on this part of the Rock. Or if there ever *have* been tracks, they are long since obliterated. It is a long long time since any living creature other than an occasional rabbit or wallaby trespassed upon its arid breast.

From Picnic at Hanging Rock *by Joan Lindsay*

14 Work with a partner to study the language used in Text 9G.

   a Paraphrase the following quotations from the passage:
- spewed red hot from the boiling bowels of the earth
- confronted by such monumental configurations of nature
- the panic exodus.

   b Find the words and phrases in the passage that stress the age of Hanging Rock, and discuss the purpose of drawing attention to this aspect of the place.

   c Find the words and phrases that personify Hanging Rock, and discuss the purpose of using this device in the passage.

15 Discuss the following aspects of Text 9G as a class:

   a the effect of the writer's use of questions

   b the effect of the writer's references to wildlife

   c the effect of including information about what the visitors cannot see.

16 a Select the words or phrases from Text 9G which suggest that the outcome of the picnic party might not be a satisfactory one.

   b What can you infer from the last sentence of the passage? Explain your interpretation of it.

   c Share with the class a prediction of what might be going to happen next in the story.

17 a Think of a place to use as a setting for a story where something mysterious or frightening happens (e.g. a disused factory or an overgrown garden).

   b Plan some ideas of how you could describe the place in a way which prefigures that something unpleasant is about to happen.

   c Write about half a page of description of your chosen place to read to the class.

   d Draft an opening and ending for your description passage, to make it a complete short story, and exchange it with a partner for comment.

   e Write a final version of your story, give it a title, and give it to your teacher.

Vocabulary building and paraphrasing are the main focus of this unit. You will be given opportunities to write a descriptive poem and a news report, and to take part in a press conference and a debate.

Activities

a List some wild animals native to your country and define each of them.

b Do a survey among your friends and family to find which wild animals, in any country, are considered to be particularly interesting or attractive in their appearance or habits. Report your findings and say why you think these animals were chosen.

c Do you think it is justified to keep wild animals in captivity? Jot down some ideas in two columns, for and against the existence of zoos.

Text 10A

Australia's feral animals

Many native species have been wiped out since the 18th century, when cats arrived on the Australian continent; it has up to 20 million **feral** cats roaming wild. Since each domestic cat is thought to catch an average of 16 mammals, 8 birds and 8 reptiles a year according to a study at the University of Adelaide, imagine how many more are being slaughtered by wild cats! Estimates suggest that they are eating more than 3500 native animals or birds a year. A strong feral cat can eat anything up to the size of a small koala.

Australian native animals are particularly vulnerable to cat predation, as they **evolved** without the defences to combat these unnatural predators which arrived on British ships originally. They also have low **reproduction** rates. When the rufus hare wallaby was reintroduced, in a short period of time it was wiped out by feral cats and now only exists in captivity. Schemes to re-establish other endangered species have also been **thwarted** in the same way.

Education of the public has caused a decline in the population of domestic cats and pet shops refuse to stock them. There is a growing feeling that people should not be allowed to keep cats near bushland areas, and that cats should be kept indoors and owners pay a registration fee. Cat lovers do not, of course, agree with these attitudes and measures just as dog lovers argue against the need to control the dingo population.

Dingoes – which also arrived by sea about 4000 years ago and are not native to Australia though they have become a national symbol – pose different threats. Because of their size, a pack can kill a fully grown kangaroo, and occasionally they attack humans. There was a **notorious** case in 1980 of a dingo apparently stealing and killing a human baby.

Many people wrongly regard dingoes as being similar to pet dogs and tourists often try to feed them, not realising that they are wild animals with a strong urge to kill. The government advice is to avoid areas where there are dingoes and never to find yourself alone amongst them. If this does happen, one should look as tall as possible and maintain eye contact with them. On no account should one run away or they will automatically chase and attack, considering you to be escaping prey.

John Parrish

2　**a**　Explain, in a single word or phrase of your own words, the meaning of each word in bold in Text 10A, as it is used in the passage.

feral　　evolved　　reproduction　　thwarted　　notorious

b　Rewrite these sentences from the passage in your own words.
　i　Australian native animals are particularly vulnerable to cat predation.
　ii　Education of the public has caused a decline in the population of domestic cats.
　iii　On no account should one run away or they will automatically chase and attack.

c　Copy and complete the Venn diagram below to show what the feral cats and the dingoes in Australia have in common and how they are different.

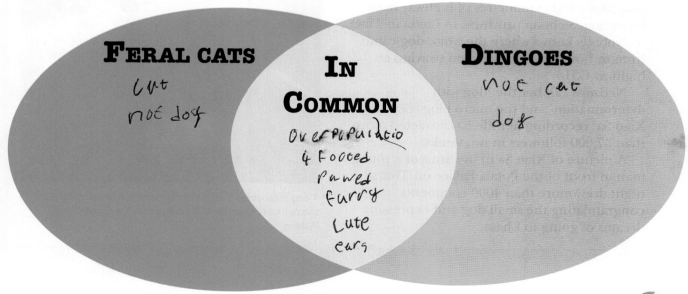

FERAL CATS
cut
not dog

IN COMMON
Overpopulatio
4 footed
Pawed
Furry
Cute
ears

DINGOES
not cat
dog

3 **a** With a partner, discuss and decide where you would put ten sets of parenthetical brackets, and add them on a copy of Text 10A. Be careful not to bracket information referred to in the next sentence.

b With a partner, decide which of the following synonyms for words in the passage evoke a stronger response by numbering them 1 to 5 to show increasing order of strength.

i	slaughter	kill	wipe out	murder	exterminate
ii	urge	feeling	compulsion	inclination	impulse
iii	prey	catch	meal	sustenance	food
iv	estimates	guesses	predictions	calculations	evaluations
v	fee	charge	cost	tax	expense

c With a partner, find as many family words (words which share a root) as you can for the following five words from the passage. If necessary, you can use a dictionary.

i   native
ii   continent
iii   captivity
iv   population
v   account

Text 10B

The stray dog who ran 1800 kilometres across China after making friends with cyclists on cross-country race

Call her a canine with a dogged determination to keep running, wherever the road may lead.

The homeless dog, known as Xiao Sa, has been following a team of cyclists for 24 days along 1833 kilometres of highway from Kangding, Sichuan province, to Lhasa in Tibet.

Nobody knows where the white dog came from or how long she has been straying on highway G318.

Netizens call her the 'dog with determination' and the micro blog 'Go Go Xiao Sa' recording her life has attracted more than 37,000 followers in two weeks.

A picture of Xiao Sa in the arms of a young man in front of the Potala Palace on Thursday night drew more than 4000 comments congratulating the small dog and expressing dreams of going to Lhasa.

A dog nicknamed Xiao Sa has become a web celebrity after she ran more than 1800 kilometres on the Qinghai-Tibet Plateau

The young man is Zhang Heng, 22, a student in Wuhan, Hubei province. As his graduation trip, he decided to face the challenge of riding to Lhasa with friends. On the way he met a lonely dog.

'She was lying, tired, on the street in Yajiang, Sichuan province,' he said. 'So we fed her, and then she followed our team.'

They thought she was following for fun, but found she insisted on sticking around them day and night.

A week later, Zhang and his buddies opened a micro blog account for her.

'We thought the dog was encouraging us, and wanted others to know its story,' he said.

They created the name Xiao Sa by combining *xiao* meaning 'little' with the last syllable of Lhasa.

During their journey, Xiao Sa, Zhang and his team covered more than 1700 kilometres and climbed ten mountains higher than 4000 metres. Xiao Sa just ran up the mountains or along dirt roads.

'Many people stopped cycling in some sections, then took the bus, but the dog made it,' he said.

Zhang put the dog on the back of the bike when the team was riding downhill.

'The speed can reach 70 kilometres per hour – impossible for the dog to catch us.'

Many other people cycling this road had learnt of the dog.

'I've heard about her from other friends who rode to Lhasa on the road before I met her,' said Wang Penghao, 24, from Jiuzhaigou, Sichuan province. 'They told me to take care of her if I saw her, and give her some food and water like they did.'

'She followed us for three days, running behind our team but sometimes leading us. She's very smart and knows the route, because she never got lost even when we passed through mountains.'

After following Wang, the dog lagged behind and met another cyclist, Wang Zi, on 4 May.

'She may be the first dog who ran to Lhasa along this route,' said Wang Zi, who was followed by the dog one day.

'I have a special feeling about her, especially when I found she was never lost, waited for us at milestones on the road, and ran all the time, making me believe that she never feels tired,' he said.

Wang Zi will continue to the foot of Qomolangma, known as Mount Everest in the West, after he arrives in Lhasa.

'If possible, I would like to take the dog with me, taking her to see a more splendid scene.'

Zhang Heng, who accompanied Xiao Sa for 20 days, called her 'a buddy and a friend'.

www.chinadaily.com.cn

4 You are going to write a shorter version of Text 10B as a news report.

a Think of other and shorter ways of expressing the title of the text.

b Discuss with a partner your alternative headlines and decide on the best. Make sure that the essential information is included, and that interest in the story has been aroused.

c On a copy of Text 10B put brackets round all the information which you do not think is essential for a news report.

d Put numbers next to the remaining information on your copy of the passage to show the most logical order to group it in, following the usual sequence for a news report.

e Write your report, under your chosen headline, making the style more concise by amalgamating the facts. Give your report to your teacher.

Text 10C

Second glance at a jaguar

Skinfull of bowls, he bowls them,
The hip going in and out of joint, dropping the spine
With the urgency of his hurry
Like a cat going along under thrown stones, under cover,
Glancing sideways, running
Under his spine. A terrible, stump-legged waddle
Like a thick Aztec disemboweller,
Club-swinging, trying to grind some square
Socket between his hind legs round,
Carrying his head like a brazier of spilling embers,
And the black bit of his mouth, he takes it
Between his back teeth, he has to wear his skin out,
He swipes a lap at the water-trough as he turns,
Swivelling the ball of his heel on the polished spot,
Showing his belly like a butterfly,
At every stride he has to turn a corner
In himself and correct it. His head
Is like the worn down stump of another whole jaguar,
His body is just the engine shoving it forward,
Lifting the air up and shoving on under,
The weight of his fangs hanging the mouth open,
Bottom jaw combing the ground. A gorged look,
Gangster, club-tail lumped along behind gracelessly,
He's wearing himself to heavy ovals,
Muttering some mantrah, some drum-song of murder
To keep his rage brightening, making his skin
Intolerable, spurred by the rosettes, the cain-brands,
Wearing the spots off from the inside,
Rounding some revenge. Going like a prayer-wheel,
The head dragging forward, the body keeping up,
The hind legs lagging. He coils, he flourishes
The blackjack tail as if looking for a target,
Hurrying through the underworld, soundless.

Ted Hughes

5 Text 10C is a poem about a caged jaguar in a zoo. Work in small
groups on the poem. Look up any words you don't know. Make notes
on the following and report back to the class.

 a Discuss the following phrases and come to an agreement about
  what you think they are saying.
   i he has to wear his skin out
   ii Swivelling the ball of his heel on the polished spot
   iii His body is just the engine shoving it forward
   iv To keep his rage brightening
   v Hurrying through the underworld

 b What shapes and colours are mentioned or implied in the poem?
  What is their effect?

 c What general impression of the jaguar is conveyed in the poem? Write
  a sentence which captures the main features of this wild animal.

Hunting snake

Sun-warmed in this late season's grace
under the autumn's gentlest sky
we walked, and froze half-through a pace.
The great black snake went reeling by.

Head-down, tongue flickering on the trail
he quested through the parting grass;
sun glazed his curves of diamond scale,
and we lost breath to watch him pass.

What track he followed, what small food
fled living from his fierce intent,
we scarcely thought; still as we stood
our eyes went with him as he went.

Cold, dark and splendid he was gone
into the grass that hid his prey.
We took a deeper breath of day,
looked at each other, and went on.

Judith Wright

6 a Comment on the poet's choice in Text 10D of the following words:

reeling   quested   splendid

b Why do you think that the snake is referred to as *he*?

c How would you describe the behaviour of the humans in this poem, and how does it differ from that of the snake?

7 a In both Texts 10C and 10D, humans are observing animal behaviour. What are the differences between the two poems? Collect some ideas and share these with the class.

b Decide which poem you prefer and think of three reasons for your preference, then share these with the class.

c Using the same metre and rhyme scheme as Text 10D, write a four-verse poem describing a wild animal of your choice which you came across while on a walk one day. Read it to the class or give it to your teacher.

Text 10E

A racehorse called Seabiscuit

A horse with bent legs and a twisted mind was a sensation on the American horse-racing circuit in the 1930s. He overcame an unlikely background and abysmal failure to electrify the nation. His blistering speed and phenomenal stamina defeated the best horses in the country and, **in fact**, shattered more than a dozen records. Thousands of fans turned out **just** to watch him exercise, and millions of radio listeners tuned in to **every one of** his races.

If his walk was **actually** so awkward it made him seem lame, his gallop was **even** more ungainly. He also had attitude problems and **more than** a fondness for sleep; Seabiscuit snoozed for hours, lying down, **indeed**, in a way **most** untypical of horses. He attacked his grooms and reacted violently to the **very** sight of a saddle or the **mere** suggestion of training.

His owner, Charles Howard, a bicycle repairman turned car distributor, teamed up with the trainer Tom Smith to 'rebuild' Seabiscuit, **not only** physically **but also** mentally. They gave him as stable companions an old pony, a stray dog and a spider monkey, and orders were given that Seabiscuit was never to be disturbed when sleeping. He began to develop an outstanding performance on the race track.

Previously one of the least successful jockeys **ever**, Reg Pollard, who could understand the minds of disturbed horses and who rode those which no one else would **so much as** go near, rode him into the record books. He discovered that Seabiscuit was disliked **even** by other horses, owing to his habit of humiliating his rivals by slowing down to mock them as he passed by, snorting in their faces and then putting on a burst of speed to win the race.

8 You are going to look closely at the language of Text 10E.

a Explain in your own words the following images from the passage:
- electrify the nation
- blistering speed
- shattered more than a dozen records.

b Look at the following phrases from Text 10E, describe their form, and explain why they are effective:
- bent legs and a twisted mind
- unlikely background and abysmal failure
- blistering speed and phenomenal stamina.

c Look at the words in bold in the passage. What is their function in the sentence?

Key point

Emphatic adverbials

The adverbs or adverbial phrases you looked at in Activity 8C could be removed from the sentence – or replaced by a simple *and* – as they have no grammatical function. Their purpose, as a stylistic device, is to make the idea being expressed more emphatic and extreme. This kind of usage is often found in journalism, which tries to create a sensational effect by exaggerating and using an excited tone.

Text 10F

File   Edit   View   History   Bookmarks   Help

The Yeti

The Himalaya Mountains, the highest range on Earth, have been referred to as the 'roof of the world'. If that is so, there is a mystery called the Yeti in our attic. This **enigma,** whose existence has never been proven, takes the shape of a hairy, biped creature that resembles a giant ape.

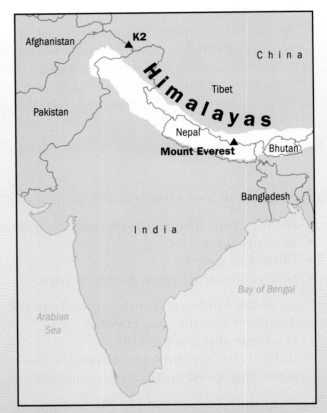

The Himalayas lie on the border between India, Nepal and China (Tibet). They are remote and forbidding. Large stretches around these rough valleys and peaks are uninhabited. The tallest mountain in the world, Everest, 8848 metres high, lies half in Nepal, half in China. It is from Nepal, though, that most attempts to climb Everest and the surrounding mountains are made. In Kathmandu, the capital of Nepal, a visitor finds himself **immersed** in the Yeti legend. It is a commercial money-maker for the tourist industry (there's even a hotel named 'The Yak and the Yeti') as well as a legend and religion to some of the Nepalese people.

The first reliable report of the Yeti appeared in 1925 when a Greek photographer, N.A. Tombazi, working as a member of a British geological expedition in the Himalayas, was shown a creature moving in the distance across some lower slopes. The creature was almost 300 metres away in an area with an altitude of around 5000 metres.

'Unquestionably, the figure in outline was exactly like a human being, walking upright and stopping occasionally to uproot some dwarf rhododendron bushes,' said Tombazi. 'It showed up dark against the snow and, as far as I could make out, wore no clothes.'

The creature disappeared before Tombazi could take a photograph, and was not seen again. As the group was descending, the photographer went out of his way to study the ground where he had spotted the creature. Tombazi found footprints in the snow.

'They were similar in shape to those of a man. The marks of five *distinct* toes and the instep were perfectly clear.'

There were 15 prints to be found. Each was about 50 cm apart. Then Tombazi lost the trail in thick brush. When the locals were asked to name the beast he'd seen, they told him it was a 'Kanchenjunga demon'. Tombazi didn't think he'd seen a demon, but he couldn't figure out what the creature was either. Perhaps he'd seen a wandering Buddhist or Hindu hermit. As the years went by and other Yeti stories surfaced, Tombazi began to wonder if that was what he too had seen.

Yeti reports usually take the form of tracks found, pelts offered, shapes seen at a distance or, rarely, actual face-to-face encounters with the creatures. These never take place with researchers looking for the Yeti, but with locals who stumble into the creature during their daily lives.

Some of the best tracks ever seen were found and photographed by British mountaineers in 1951. They found them on the south-western slopes of the Menlung Glacier, which lies between Tibet and Nepal, at an altitude of 6000 metres. The tracks seemed fresh and the mountaineers followed the trail until it disappeared in hard ice. Some scientists who viewed the photographs could not identify the tracks as belonging to any known creature. Others, though, felt it was probably the trail of a langur monkey or red bear. They pointed out that tracks in snow, melted by the sun, can change shape and grow larger, and the footprints were explained by this fact. Even so, the bear/monkey theory seems unlikely to be true, as both of these animals normally move on all four feet. These tracks were clearly those of a biped.

These footprints were not the first or last discovered by climbers in the Himalayas. Even Sir Edmund Hillary and his Sherpa guide, Tenzing Norgay, on their record *ascent* to the top of Mount Everest in 1953, found giant footprints on their way up.

One of the more **curious** reports of a close encounter with a Yeti occurred in 1938. Captain d'Auvergue, the curator of the Victoria Memorial in Kolkata, India, was travelling in the Himalayas by himself when he became snowblind. As he neared death from exposure he was rescued by a three-metre tall Yeti that nursed him back to health until d'Auvergue was able to return home by himself.

In many other stories, though, the Yeti hasn't been so *benign*. One Sherpa girl, who was tending her yaks, described being surprised by a large ape-like creature with black and brown hair. It started to drag her off, but seemed to be distracted by her screams and let her go. It then **savagely** attacked and killed two of her yaks. She escaped with her life and the incident was reported to the police, who found footprints.

Several expeditions have been organised to track down the Yeti, but none has discovered anything more than footprints and **questionable** artefacts like scalps and hides. A theory recently suggested is that the Yeti is actually three animals: the rare Tibetan blue bear which attacks cattle; a gibbon that may live as far north as Nepal, though it's never been spotted past the Brahmaputra River in India; a mysterious savage ape covered with black or red hair that can live at altitudes of up to 6000 metres.

So far there is no firm evidence to *support* the existence of the Yeti, but there is none to show that it doesn't exist either. If it indeed becomes known that such a creature lives in the *barren*, frozen, upper reaches of the Himalayas where few men dare to tread, the Yeti may find its refuge safe for a long time to come.

Lee Krystek

9 **a** Give a synonym for each word in bold in Text 10F, as it is used in the passage.

enigma   immersed   curious   savagely   questionable

b Give an antonym (opposite) for each word in italics in Text 10F, as it is used in the passage.

distinct   ascent   benign   support   barren

c Say whether the following statements about the Yeti are true or false, according to the passage.
   i   The Yeti walks on two feet.
   ii Some Nepalese people do not believe in the Yeti.
   iii The first photographs of footprints were taken in 1953.
   iv The Yeti is thought to kill animals.
   v   The Yeti lives at altitudes above 6000 metres.

10 Read the tip on the next page, then complete this activity with a partner.

a Give phrasal verbs with *come* to replace the following verbs used in Text 10F.
   ● appeared
   ● found
   ● stumble into

b Give phrasal verbs with *put* to replace the following verbs used in the passage.
   ● distracted
   ● suggested
   ● went out of his way

c Give phrasal verbs with *turn* to replace the following verbs used in the passage.
   ● surfaced
   ● attacked
   ● becomes known

For Activity 10
Phrasal verbs with *come, put* and *turn*

These are three of the most common verbs from which phrasal verbs are made. They cover a wide range of meanings and with different prepositions are synonyms for many other verbs. The test of whether a verb is a phrasal verb, or just a verb with a preposition which always or usually follows it, is to remove the preposition and see if the verb then loses its particular meaning: for example, *to look at* is a verb plus preposition, but *to look after* has a specific figurative meaning and cannot be split. The three verbs *come, put* and *turn* are not normally followed by any particular preposition and their meaning when they stand alone is very general, whereas *come round* (regain consciousness), *put up with* (tolerate) or *turn out* (various meanings) all have very specific meanings.

11 Your class is going to hold a press conference on the subject of the existence of the Yeti.

a The class is divided into explorers (about four) and journalists. The explorers need to work as a group to decide on the details of a trip they have just made to the Himalayas, where they saw a strange creature which they believe to be a Yeti. The journalists need to work in a group or groups to decide which questions each of them will ask the team or teams of explorers. Both explorers and journalists need to collect evidence from Text 10F to use in their questions and answers (and you may do some further online research of the topic first).

b Extra details can be added to questions and answers and ideas inferred from the passage, such as measurements and descriptions of the creature, and geographical and time references.

c Simulate the press conference, with the teacher as organiser. Everyone should get a chance to speak. Journalists and explorers should make notes during the role play.

12 a Now plan a news report, using the notes you made in Activity 11c, under the headline 'Everest climbers claim Yeti sighting'.

b Write or type your news report (including an appropriate graphic).

c Exchange your report with a partner to check for accuracy, and then give it to your teacher.

13 Now you are going to prepare for and participate in a debate about zoos. First read the key point on the next page.

a The class is divided into two, four or six roughly equal groups, depending on the size of the class. Half of the class will prepare speeches arguing that zoos should exist, the other half that they should not.

b In your group, plan a speech for or against zoos, referring back to the notes you made in Activity 1c, and adding supporting evidence from your own experiences of zoos you have visited (both in your own country and overseas) and your own knowledge of wild animals and the issues concerning them. You may be given some time to research online.

c Two or three speakers are elected for each side, and the rest of their group help them to practise the structure and delivery of their speeches, which should include all the ideas collected in the group.

d The debate is held, with alternating speakers for and against the motion 'This House believes that zoos are necessary.' Questions may be asked of the speakers by the non-speakers after all the speeches have been delivered. A vote is taken at the end by the non-speakers.

e Write a summary of the ideas used on both sides, organising the ideas into 'for' and 'against' arguments. Check it and give it to your teacher.

Key point

Debating

The number of speakers representing the groups can vary according to class size, but there should be at least two speakers 'for' the motion (the 'proposers') and two speakers 'against' the motion, who speak alternately, beginning with a speaker 'for'. The proposers are supported by 'seconders'. You may not be able to be on the side you personally believe in; in real life people often have to argue a case which they do not actually support.

Effective debate speeches contain various kinds of supporting evidence: recent events reported in the media; statistics; quotations by members of relevant organisations; references to personal experience. Effective debate speakers are those who can speak clearly, fluently and persuasively, without getting lost or repeating themselves, and using eye contact with the audience rather than reading from their script all the time.

The voting at the end should be according to which case was presented more persuasively, and not according to what you believe, or which team you were working for, or who your friends are among the speakers!

UNIT 11 Music and dance

In this unit you will learn more about effective description, and focus on vocabulary extension, revision of tense and use of the passive, time adverbs and prepositions, and negative phrasing for emphasis. You will read a review, a plot synopsis and a poem, and write a formal letter and a description of a performance you have seen.

Activities

1 **a** List all the different musical instruments you can think of, grouping them under the headings 'stringed', 'wind', 'percussion' and 'keyboard'.

   b Discuss in class which musical instrument you like to play or listen to, and try to explain your preference.

   c Think about the types of music and dance which are traditional to your country. How would you describe their characteristics?

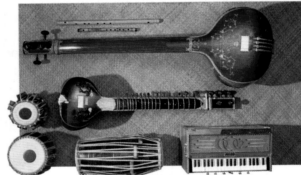

2 In this activity you will look closely at some of the vocabulary in Text 11A.

   a The words in bold in the passage are used metaphorically. Use them in sentences of your own to show their literal meanings. You may need to check them in a dictionary first.

   infectious   unbridled   palpable   powerhouse   freak of nature

   b The words below are from the passage. Copy them in your notebook. Join with a line the words on the left to the correct synonym in the list on the right.

   exuberant   boisterous
   sombre   enthusiastic
   flamboyant   serious
   raucous   strong
   intense   showy

   c The following words from the passage are specialist terms used in the context of the performance arts (music, dance and drama). Define them in your own words.

   orchestra   standing ovation   auditorium   encore   repertoire

Text 11A

The Simón Bolívar Youth Orchestra

This week the Simón Bolívar Youth Orchestra from Venezuela hit town in a blaze of colour, excitement and glamour – qualities <u>not often associated</u> with the world of classical music. The Festival Hall on Tuesday witnessed scenes of Boli-mania <u>not seen since</u> the orchestra's last visit to Britain in 2007, when they set the place alight, owing to their **infectious joy**, exuberant antics and **unbridled** enthusiasm for making music. The audience gave the youngsters a standing ovation; children screamed and adults squealed with delight at the end of the concert.

After an essentially sombre, if exciting, programme, we were all hoping for some colour in the encores, and boy did we get it! The hall suddenly went dark, the orchestra put on their colourful Venezuelan jackets over their black dresses or suits, and the place went wild. As the youngsters launched into the first of two encores, both flamboyant Latin American classics that form part of their repertoire, we were <u>no longer</u> in a damp, grey London but in a raucous Latin America of the spirit. They stood up, shimmied, danced and threw their instruments in the air, before hurling their jackets into the auditorium. They had clearly done it <u>no end of</u> times before, but the pleasure they took in it was **palpable**.

The sound they make is immense and intense; owing to the 180 young faces full of concentration and pleasure, the classical music they make feels incredibly vital. The inspiration and passion of this music, being played as if their lives depended upon it, is due to love, honesty and commitment.

The 28-year-old conductor is a **powerhouse**, owing to the fact that he jumps on the spot to encourage the orchestra, his hair waving wildly, every bone of his body bending to the notes.

The Simón Bolívar orchestra is <u>no **freak of nature**</u> – it is the product of a 34-year-old project run by the Venezuelan government which gives every girl and boy, however poor, the chance to have <u>not only</u> free music tuition <u>but</u> an instrument. The result is that <u>no fewer than</u> a quarter of a million children – three quarters of them below the poverty line – are involved in making music in hundreds of orchestras. The Simón Bolívar Youth Orchestra are ambassadors for a philosophy, a way of life. Given the widespread contempt in which classical music is held by teenagers in this country, you couldn't help feeling that attendance at one of these life-affirming events should be <u>nothing less than</u> compulsory.

Paul Gent, Daily Telegraph

3 **a** Study the use of these negative phrases, underlined in Text 11A, and discuss in class the reason for their use and their overall effect in the passage.

not often associated	no freak of nature
not seen since	not only . . . but
no longer	no fewer than
no end of	nothing less than

b On a copy of Text 11A, underline all the uses of triple structure in the passage, and describe in each case the structure being repeated, e.g. adjective plus noun.

c Use the following descriptive writing clichés, used in the passage, as a writing frame for a paragraph describing a music or dance event. Then read it to the class.

. . . a blaze of . . . witnessed scenes of . . . set the place alight . . . the place went wild . . . as if their lives depended upon it . . . you couldn't help feeling . . .

Text 11B on the next page is about Mimi, a very young pianist.

4 **a** Rewrite Text 11B as a one-paragraph press statement for the concert, then read it to the class.

For Activity 4a
Press statements

A press statement is a purely informative notification of an event which has happened or is about to happen. It contains all the relevant facts and a brief explanation of why the occasion is significant. A press statement is a kind of summary and does not include quotations, opinions, background details or comparisons.

b Look at the hyphenated words in Text 11B. With a partner, remind yourselves of the rule for hyphen usage, and decide where to put hyphens in the groups of words below.
  i four year old piano playing genius
  ii solo performance artist and classically trained musician
  iii prize winning and internationally renowned jazz player
  iv two year programme of one hour lessons twice weekly
  v world class guitarist and ex band leader

Text 11B

Four-year-old prodigy

Most four-year-olds are content with banging on a drum and would struggle to get a note out of a recorder. But child prodigy Mimi Zou has astounded her piano teacher with her progress and tomorrow night will give her first solo performance in London's Royal Albert Hall.

Mimi, who has been learning the piano for only a year, is flying from her home in China to perform. She was discovered by teachers of the reception class at an international school in Tianjin. She had been taught by a local Chinese woman, and was already playing grade-five-standard pieces.

Steven Griffiths, the musical director of the school, says, 'She is not nervous at all. I have never seen anything like this before. She can read music. She isn't just copying what she is shown.'

Speaking on behalf of Mimi's family, who do not speak English, Mr Griffiths said: 'She practises for three hours a day, and I give her a 40-minute lesson once a week. I am feeling my way really, because I have never taught a four-year-old before.

'Her mother sits in on the lessons so she can see what Mimi is doing, and we have a translator. She is not perfect yet and has a long way to go, but if she is handled well she has a great future.'

Mimi, who took to playing the piano after watching her 11-year-old brother Andy practising, said that her favourite composers were Mozart and Bach. Andy has since given up the piano, after being so overshadowed by his little sister.

A spokesman for the Royal Albert Hall said Mimi was almost certainly the youngest pianist to perform solo there. Tonight, she will take centre-stage in front of thousands of pupils and past students of the school, and will perform from memory a two-minute solo piece in the style of a Chinese national dance, by Chinese composer Lvding He.

Mozart is believed to have started playing the keyboard at the age of three, and was composing by five. By the time he was 11, he had composed his first opera.

www.standard.co.uk

c With a partner, look at the three pairs of sentences below and decide which one is correct in each pair, the one with the comma or the one without, and why. Look at the key point below to check you are right.

    i   'Mimi, will you play something for us?'
        'Mimi will you play something for us?'

    ii Four-year-old Mimi, will give her first performance tomorrow.
        Four-year-old Mimi will give her first performance tomorrow.

    iii Mimi wanted to learn the piano, after watching her brother practising.
        Mimi wanted to learn the piano after watching her brother practising.

Key point

More about commas

Another application of commas – but still covered by the overall rule that 'if it can be removed, comma it' – is to show when a person is being addressed directly by a speaker. If the name of the person being addressed is given in direct speech, then it must have commas before and after (depending on where it is in the sentence) to show that the name is not part of the content of the speech but an indication of who is being spoken to or a way of attracting their attention (see the pair of sentences in part i above).

It is important that a comma should not be used if it separates a subject from its verb, as in example ii above (unless two commas are being used to form a 'removable' parenthesis), or if a clause is defining a person or action and is therefore an integral part of the meaning, as in example iii.

In the next two activities you will look closely at the verbs and time adverbs in Text 11B.

 a The following phrasal verbs occur in Text 11B:

    sit in on   took to   given up

Give other examples of phrasal verbs based on *sit, take* and *give*, and use them in sentences which show their meaning.

b   The first two paragraphs of the passage contain verbs in nine forms.
    Copy and complete the table. For each verb, say what the tense is
    called, whether it is active or passive, and what the rule is for its use.

Verb	Tense	Active or passive	Rule for use of this tense
are content			
would struggle			
has astounded			
will give			
has been learning			
is flying			
was discovered			
had been taught			
was playing			

c   With a partner, look at the tenses of the verbs in the following
    sentences. Copy out the sentences and choose the appropriate time
    adverb to complete them. Use the key point below to help you.

    ago   already   at   by   for   from   since   still

    i   She has been learning the piano ___ a year.
    ii   She started learning the piano a year ___.
    iii   She has been learning the piano ___ last year.
    iv   She started playing the piano ___ the age of three.
    v   She had started playing the piano ___ the time she was three.
    vi   She was ___ playing the violin when she was three.
    vii   She was ___ playing the violin when she was thirteen.
    viii She has played the violin ___ the age of three.

Key point

Past time indicators

These time adverbs determine the tense of the verb which accompanies
them and the meaning of the action within a time frame. For example:

She played the piano a year **ago**, *but she doesn't play it any more.*

It is helpful to draw a timeline labelled *past perfect*, *past* and *present*,
and place the adverbs on it to indicate which of them show an action
that:
*   started in the past perfect and continued into the past
*   started in the past and is now finished
*   started in the past and is still continuing
*   started in the past and it is not clear whether it is still continuing.

6   **a**   Write these sentences as active constructions.
- **i**   Mozart is believed to have started playing at the age of three.
- **ii**   She was discovered by teachers of the reception class.
- **iii** If she is handled well she has a great future.

     b   Say why you think the verbs are used in the passage in the passive form.

     c   Write a letter to the Minister for the Arts in your country, explaining why you believe that every child should have the chance to have free music lessons from an early age. Use ideas from Texts 11A and 11B in your letter, and also add some of your own. Use passive verb forms where appropriate.

Text 11C on the next page is about Carlos Acosta, the Cuban ballet dancer.

7   **a**   Text 11C contains some colloquial and idiomatic expressions. Rewrite the following phrases in a more formal way.
- **i**   I'm pretty laid-back about clothes
- **ii**   I love to hang out with my family
- **iii** it was like 'Wow!'
- **iv** everybody needs their own space
- **v**   it's a very cool feeling

     b   Note that in the passage 'all right' is written as two words. Copy the ten 'words' below and add slashes (/) to show which of them split into more than one word, and where.

       nearby   altogether   nevertheless   insofaras   everywhere
       themselves   alotof   always   furthermore   inbetween

     c   Rewrite the following groups of simple sentences from the passage, joining each set into one complex sentence in as many ways as possible.
- **i**   Most of the time I wear T-shirts and casual stuff. I have a couple of expensive designer suits for black-tie functions. I don't like wearing them.
- **ii**   I have the book inside my head. I know exactly where I'm going. You discover things about the characters which set up new possibilities.
- **iii** We eat a late dinner at home. Charlotte does the cooking. I can only make black beans with rice.

Text 11C

A day in the life of Carlos Acosta, 36, the Cuban ballet dancer

I eat breakfast at 8.30 – oatmeal, bananas, mangoes, papayas and tea. And owing to the need for protein, I often have eggs as well. I'm pretty laid-back about clothes. Most of the time I wear T-shirts and casual stuff. I have a couple of expensive designer suits for black-tie functions. I don't like wearing them, but sometimes you have to dress up.

In Havana, I sit on my terrace while I eat breakfast, looking out at white sand. The sea is four blocks away. When I'm away, not being able to see a blue sky every day makes me miserable. It's good to have someone to come home to. Charlotte is a writer. We lead an ordinary life – shopping, going to movies, getting my hair cut! And I love to hang out with my family.

Ballet is like training for the Olympics eight hours a day, and when you're performing you have to take classes. We break for an hour at 12 for lunch in the canteen. It's not good to overeat, because after lunch you work on the repertoire and you know you're going to have to jump. Flying in the air feels amazing. When I was younger and could be up there with nothing hurting it was like 'Wow!' The older you get, the more you need ice packs and massage, which I have at least twice a week.

Life in Havana is hectic. I'm happy to teach at the National Ballet School when they ask me. Owing to my experiences travelling and performing, I bring a melting pot of different cultures and influences to my teaching. I know a lot of people in Cuba, but many from my group have left. Things change. Everyone wants the opportunity to make a better life and earn money. My security is due to the property I've bought and the sound investments I've made.

I always suffer from jetlag. I travel a lot with Charlotte, but not when I'm rehearsing. Then I have to clear my head to concentrate on learning choreography. Sometimes I need to be alone. Everybody needs their own space. I work on a laptop in my messy dressing room, where I'm able to cut myself off from everything. I am writing a novel in Spanish. I have the book inside my head and I know exactly where I'm going. But in the process of writing, things happen. You discover things about the characters which set up new possibilities. When the writing goes all right, it's a very cool feeling.

We eat a late dinner at home. Charlotte does the cooking. I can only make black beans with rice, which we eat a lot in Cuba. I throw off my shoes. It's wonderful to pad about barefoot on the wooden floor, but dancers have such ugly feet!

Sunday Times Magazine

In Text 11D the full stops and commas have been removed.

Text 11D

Every Body Is Doing It

In Hawaii they Hula
They Tango in Argentina
They Reggae in Jamaica
And they Rumba down in Cuba
In Trinidad and Tobago
They do the Calypso
And in Spain the Spanish
They really do Flamenco

In the Punjab they Bhangra
How they dance Kathak in India
Over in Guatemala
They dance the sweet Marimba
Even foxes dance a lot
They invented the Fox Trot
In Australia it's true
They dance to the Didgeridoo

In Kenya they Benga
They Highlife in Ghana
They dance Ballet all over
And Rai dance in Algeria
They Jali in Mali
In Brazil they Samba
And the girls do Belly Dancing
In the northern parts of Africa

Everybody does the Disco
From Baghdad to San Francisco
Many folk with razzamataz
Cannot help dancing to Jazz
They do the Jig in Ireland
And it is really true
They still Morris dance in England
When they can find time to

Benjamin Zephaniah

8   **a** Working with a partner, add punctuation to a copy of Text 11D.

   b Look at the rhyme in the poem. Is there a regular pattern? How would you describe the kind of rhymes being used? Use the tip below to help you.

   c Add an extra verse to the poem, mentioning other dances, music and countries. Use rhyming couplets and alternate rhyme, and try to include some half-rhymes too. Read out your extra lines to the class.

For Activity 8b
Half-rhyme

When words do not really rhyme but have similar vowel sounds and the same consonants (consonance) we call it half-rhyme. It can have a cheerful effect, as here, or a poignant one because of the echoes and discord it creates, as in the half-rhymes of *soul* and *all*, *frowned* and *friend*. Half-rhymes allow a more subtle range of rhyming effects, especially when combined with other rhyming schemes, and help to avoid the sing-song chiming of full rhymes.

Text 11E on the next page is a synopsis (plot summary) of the musical *Evita* by Andrew Lloyd Webber and Tim Rice.

9   **a** Explain in your own words the meaning of the five idiomatic phrases in bold in Text 11E. The meanings can be inferred from the context.
   i   her native Argentina   iv high society
   ii lowly birth   v   better the lot of
   iii fall foul of

   b As in Text 11A, negative forms are used in the passage for positive effect (e.g. *not many*, meaning *a few*, a device called litotes, which is a kind of irony). Find five examples of this usage in Text 11E and give their positive form.

   c Copy and complete this sentence to summarise the life story of Evita, as described in the passage.

   Eva Perón was a famous Argentinian who . . .

File   Edit   View   History   Bookmarks   Help

Evita

This musical tells the story of Eva (Evita) Perón (1919–52), a woman whose name evokes powerful feelings in **her native Argentina**. It begins with the news of Evita's death, and then turns to a much earlier scene at her father's funeral. Eva was the child (one of many) of a rural landowner and her seamstress mother. Hers was not a wealthy childhood by any means, and she was continually discriminated against because of her **lowly birth**. She is refused admission to her father's funeral for this reason. This scene is contrasted with her own funeral, a spectacular affair not different from that of a beloved head of state.

Eva leaves her village at the age of 15 to go to Buenos Aires and begin her campaign to become a performer, actress and public figure. In 1944 she meets Juan Perón, an ambitious young army officer, who is imprisoned when he **falls foul of** the government of the time, which was far from liberal. Eva possesses persuasive skills and she uses her position as a celebrity to get him released. Following their marriage, she remains a formidable supporter, her help proving crucial to his later becoming the head of state.

Once Juan Perón becomes the president of Argentina, Eva expects better treatment from Argentina's **high society**, but they snub her without mercy. She, in response, diverts government money from society-led charities and starts the Eva Perón Foundation. As its president, she works tirelessly and continuously to **better the lot of** Argentina's poor. For this work, and for having risen from poor origins to glory, she is beloved by huge masses of her fellow citizens, if not by those of high rank. She also arranges for women in Argentina to get the vote. Her death from cancer at the age of 33, while at the height of her power and influence, strikes the whole world as tragic.

The most celebrated song from this musical of Evita's life is 'Don't Cry For Me, Argentina'.

Clarke Fountain, Rovi

10 **a** Use these words from Text 11E in sentences of your own to show you understand their meaning.

> discriminated   formidable   crucial   snub   tragic

b The following five words from the passage are often misspelt. Write them out with their 'hot spots' underlined. Then write them three times each without looking at the word. Check that you spelt them correctly.

> scene   campaign   government   possesses   height

c The words *continually* and *continuously* are both used in the passage. They are often confused. Look at their context and see if you can define their different meanings. Then read the key point below to check you are right.

Key point

Continual and **continuous**

Continual means that something is happening on and off with breaks in between (e.g. 'There was the continual noise of trains going past'). *Continuous* means that something is happening without any breaks (e.g. 'There was a continuous noise of a burglar alarm going off').

11 With a partner, choose one of the photographs on the next page to describe.

a Study closely your chosen photograph of dancers and make notes of words and phrases to describe the setting and movements of the performance.

b Imagine a conversation between two people watching the dance. Write a dialogue for what they might say to each other (e.g. how difficult the dance is, what is interesting about it). Include your notes from Activity 11a.

c Read out your dialogue to the class.

12 Your task is to write a description, of about a page, of a dance or music performance that you have seen either live or on screen. Use the guidance in the key point on page 169, and look back at Text 11A to help you. Plan, draft, write and check your description, then give it to your teacher.

Key point

More about descriptive writing

- Descriptions can be written in sentences of any length – a variety is recommended – but they do need to be in sentences, i.e. to contain a finite verb, and not a series of verbless notes.

- Although the main focus of descriptive writing is adjectives – notice how many are used in Text 11A – verbs are also a valuable vehicle for conveying description. Verbs in descriptive writing tend to be stronger than their purely informative synonyms, for instance *hurled* is used rather than *thrown*, and *launched into* for *started*.

- The aim of reviewing a performance is to make the reader feel part of a dramatic event and powerful atmosphere, and all parts of speech contribute to the creation of the whole picture.

- Descriptive pieces need a structure of some kind, otherwise they sound like random lists and it is difficult for the reader to get an overall sense of the shape of what is being described.

- They do not, however, need paragraph links of the kind used in discursive and argumentative writing, such as *secondly*, *furthermore* and *nevertheless*. Nor do they need the chronology links used in narrative, such as *meanwhile* and *after some time*.

- Description sometimes relies on a recurring image to give it structure. There is recurring reference to the idea of fire in Text 11A, which conveys the colourfulness and excitement of the performance.

- Another common descriptive stylistic device is the use of three grammatical structures together, for example 'infectious joy, exuberant antics and unbridled enthusiasm'; 'a blaze of colour, excitement and glamour'. More than three becomes list-like and only two is less effective, so three is considered the perfect number for richness of description as well as elegance of expression.

- Pairing of words which sound similar, as well as those connected by assonance and alliteration (e.g. 'every bone of his body bending'), is a way of making description more powerful, as in 'immense and intense'.

- Don't forget about the use of negative forms to create stronger positive effects (e.g. *no fewer than*, *tirelessly*, *not unrelated*).

UNIT 12 A load of nonsense

This unit focuses on nonsense verse and prose, coined words, pronunciation and spelling anomalies. Ways of expressing the future are discussed. You will practise describing pictures and processes, using dialogue and reported speech, and giving a presentation.

Activities

1 **a** List your favourite nonsense poems, songs or stories, including those containing made-up creatures; they may be those you read or heard as a young child, perhaps as nursery rhymes.

   b Share with the class any made-up words you know, maybe from songs or advertisements (e.g. *supercalifragilisticexpialidocious*, *gubbins*, *tickety-boo*, *widget*). Discuss the purpose and appeal of nonsense words.

   c List all the humorous poems, cartoons and stories you can think of. Discuss the relationship between humour and nonsense.

This is an extract from a nonsense poem called 'The Hunting of the Snark'.

Text 12A

There was also a Beaver, that paced on the deck,
   Or would sit making lace in the bow:
And had often (the Bellman said) saved them from wreck
   Though none of the sailors knew how.

> There was one who was famed for the number of things
>   He forgot when he entered the ship:
> His umbrella, his watch, all his jewels and rings,
>   And the clothes he had bought for the trip.
>
> He had forty-two boxes, all carefully packed,
>   With his name painted clearly on each:
> But, since he omitted to mention the fact,
>   They were all left behind on the beach.
>
> The loss of his clothes hardly mattered, because
>   He had seven coats on when he came,
> With three pairs of boots – but the worst of it was,
>   He had wholly forgotten his name.
>
> He would answer to 'Hi!' or to any loud cry,
>   Such as 'Fry me!' or 'Fritter my wig!'
> To 'What-you-may-call-um!' or 'What-was-his-name!'
>   But especially 'Thing-um-a-jig!'
>
> *Lewis Carroll*

2 Discuss the following aspects of Text 12A with a partner.

a Reread the poem and list all the absurdities about the sailor (referred to as 'one').

b *Thing-um-a-jig* is a nonsense word for *thing* (usually written nowadays as *thingummyjig*). What other words can you think of which people use when they can't remember the name of the thing they are trying to refer to?

c Judging from its name, what kind of creature do you imagine a 'snark' to be?

3 With a partner, look more closely at the vocabulary in Text 12A.

a There are words in English that are spelt the same but have two different pronunciations depending on their meaning or tense. These are known as homographs. An example in Text 12A is *bow* in the first verse, in which the vowel can be pronounced as either /əʊ/ (as in *slow*) or /aʊ/ (as in *how*). List as many other homographs as you can think of.

b The words *wreck* and *wholly* in the poem extract have an initial silent *w*. List as many other words as you can which begin with or contain a silent *w*.

c Look at the number *forty-two* at the beginning of the third verse of the poem extract. What is surprising about the way it is spelt? Which other numbers change their spelling when made into a teen number or multiple of ten?

4 **a** Look at the illustration above of a crazy invention. What do you think it is?

b Discuss in class why it is amusing.

c In a list of numbered stages, describe how it works. With a partner, compare your descriptions.

5 With a partner, think of an idea for a new invention.

  a Decide on a design for a machine which will perform a task.

  b Draw a diagram to show how it works.

  c Draw or project your diagram on to the board and explain to the class how your invention works.

Text 12B is a rap poem. It uses non-standard English.

Write-A-Rap Rap

Hey, everybody, let's write a rap.
First there's a rhythm you'll need to clap.
Keep that rhythm and stay in time,
'cause a rap needs rhythm and a good strong rhyme.

The rhyme keeps coming in the very same place
so don't fall behind and try not to race.
The rhythm keeps the rap on a regular beat
and the rhyme helps to wrap your rap up neat.

'But what'll we write?' I hear you shout.
There ain't no rules for what a rap's about.
You can rap about a robber, you can rap about a king,
You can rap about a chewed up piece of string . . .
(well, you can rap about almost . . . anything!)

You can rap about the ceiling, you can rap about the floor,
you can rap about the window, write a rap on the door.
You can rap about things that are mean or pleasant,
you can rap about wrapping up a Christmas present.

You can rap about a mystery hidden in a box,
you can rap about a pair of smelly old socks.
You can rap about something that's over and gone,
you can rap about something going on and on and on and on . . .

But when you think there just ain't nothing left to say . . .
you can wrap it all up and put it away.
It's a rap. It's a rap. It's a rap rap rap rap RAP!

Tony Mitton

6 a In what ways is Text 12B a kind of nonsense?

  b Find the non-standard English words in the poem and write their full or usual forms.

  c Discuss in class why certain kinds of text use non-standard English, giving examples. The tip below will help you.

Tip

For Activity 6c
Non-standard English

Non-standard English contains words or grammar formations which are spelt or pronounced differently from standard written English, and which often include contractions. It is used by writers when they want to make their writing sound conversational because the characters and situation are informal. Sometimes the aim of breaking the rules is to be amusing, or to appeal to a particular audience, such as teenagers or young children. Be careful when writing exam responses not to use such language.

7 a In class decide on a definition of a rap, judging from the characteristics of the poem.

  b Using the same form as the poem, write your own rap on any subject of your choice, beginning 'Hey everybody, this is a rap!'

  c Perform your rap to the class. Give feedback on each other's poems and performances.

Text 12C on the next page comes from the nonsensical novel *Alice's Adventures in Wonderland* by Lewis Carroll.

8 a List the different kinds of punctuation used in the poem.

  b On a copy of Text 12C, underline all the personal pronouns used in the poem. What is the effect of the use of so many?

  c Listen to the poem being read aloud in a way which observes all the punctuation marks. Discuss how you think the punctuation adds to the humour and absurdity of the poem.

9 a Describe in one sentence what is surreal about the picture in Text 12C.

  b Text 12C is nonsense in a different way from both Texts 12A and 12B. Why is this a nonsense poem? *this text can only be understood will aditinal information which is witaheld from the reader*

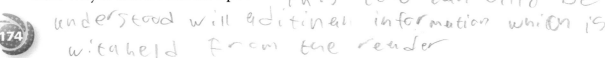

c How easy do you think it is to write this kind of nonsense? Try to
write another verse for the poem in the same format.

Text 12C

'They told me you had been to her,
    And mentioned me to him:
She gave me a good character,
    But said I could not swim.

He sent them word I had not gone
    (We know it to be true):
If she should push the matter on,
    What would become of you?

I gave her one, they gave him two,
    You gave us three or more;
They all returned from him to you,
    Though they were mine before.

If I or she should chance to be
    Involved in this affair,
He trusts to you to set them free,
    Exactly as we were.

My notion was that you had been
    (Before she had this fit)
An obstacle that came between
    Him, and ourselves, and it.

Don't let him know she liked them best,
    For this must ever be
A secret, kept from all the rest,
    Between yourself and me.'

Text 12D on the next page is a poem about a made-up creature.

10 a Draw a picture of the Snitterjipe from the description in Text 12D.

b There are many fictional creatures in children's literature (e.g. elf,
dragon, goblin, unicorn, mermaid). Make up a new one and write a
dictionary definition description of it.

c Now make up a non-existent name, like Snitterjipe, for your new creature. It should have a sound which matches its appearance, character or habits.

Text 12D

The Snitterjipe

In mellow orchards, rich and ripe,
Is found the luminous Snitterjipe.
Bad boys who climb the bulging trees
Feel his sharp breath about their knees;
His trembling whiskers tickle so,
They squeak and squeal till they let go.
They hear his far-from-friendly bark;
They see his eyeballs in the dark
Shining and shifting in their sockets
As round and big as pears in pockets.
They feel his hot and wrinkly hide;
They see his nostrils flaming wide,
His tapering teeth, his jutting jaws,
His tongue, his tail, his twenty claws.
His hairy shadow in the moon,
It makes them sweat, it makes them swoon;
And as they climb the orchard wall,
They let their pilfered **pippins** fall.
The Snitterjipe suspends pursuit
And falls upon the fallen fruit;
And while they flee the monster fierce,
Apples, not boys, his talons pierce.
With thumping hearts they hear him munch—
Six apples at a time he'll crunch.
At length he falls asleep, and they
On tiptoe take their homeward way.
But long before the blackbirds pipe
To welcome day, the Snitterjipe
Has fled afar, and on the green
Only his fearsome prints are seen.

James Reeves

| **pippin** | a type of apple |

11 **a** What are the most striking features of the language in Text 12D, and what is their effect?

b What is the rhyme and metre of the poem? What is the effect of its regularity?

c Add some more descriptive couplets to the Snitterjipe, in the same rhyme and metre, which are alliterative and contain assonance. Read them to the class.

Text 12E is an extract from *Alice's Adventures in Wonderland*. Alice meets a surreal cat which can disappear, leaving only its smile.

She was a little startled by seeing the Cheshire Cat sitting on a bough of a tree a few yards off.

The Cat only grinned when it saw Alice. It looked good-natured, she thought: still it had *very* long claws and a great many teeth, so she felt that it ought to be treated with respect.

'Cheshire Puss,' she began, rather timidly, as she did not at all know whether it would like the name: however, it only grinned a little wider.

'Come, it's pleased so far,' thought Alice, and she went on. 'Would you tell me, please, which way I ought to go from here?'

'That depends a good deal on where you want to get to,' said the Cat.

'I don't much care where—' said Alice.

'Then it doesn't matter which way you go,' said the Cat.

'—so long as I get *somewhere*,' Alice added as an explanation.

'Oh, you're sure to do that,' said the Cat, 'if you only walk long enough.'

Alice felt that this could not be denied, so she tried another question.

'What sort of people live about here?'

'In *that* direction,' the Cat said, waving its right paw round, 'lives a Hatter: and in *that* direction,' waving the other paw, 'lives a March Hare. Visit either you like: they're both mad.'

'But I don't want to go among mad people,' Alice remarked.

'Oh, you can't help that,' said the Cat: 'we're all mad here. I'm mad. You're mad.'

'How do you know I'm mad?' said Alice.

'You must be,' said the Cat, 'or you wouldn't have come here.'

Alice didn't think that proved it at all; however, she went on: 'And how do you know that you're mad?'

'To begin with,' said the Cat, 'a dog's not mad. You grant that?'

'I suppose so,' said Alice.

'Well, then,' the Cat went on, 'you see, a dog growls when it's angry, and wags its tail when it's pleased. Now I growl when I'm pleased, and wag my tail when I'm angry. Therefore I'm mad.'

'I call it purring, not growling,' said Alice.

'Call it what you like,' said the Cat. 'Do you play croquet with the Queen to-day?'

'I should like it very much,' said Alice, 'but I haven't been invited yet.'

'You'll see me there,' said the Cat, and vanished.

Lewis Carroll

12 Can you agree with a partner what is nonsensical about the dialogue in Text 12E? Think about:

a the relationship between the speakers

b the order of the dialogue

c the content of the dialogue.

13 a Rewrite as reported speech the following extract from Text 12E, remembering the rules for changing person and tense, and time and place references.

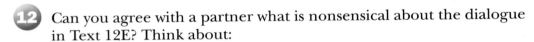

Alice went on, 'Would you tell me, please, which way I ought to go from here?'

'That depends a good deal on where you want to get to,' said the Cat.

'I don't much care where—' said Alice.

'Then it doesn't matter which way you go,' said the Cat.

'—so long as I get *somewhere*,' Alice added as an explanation.

'Oh, you're sure to do that,' said the Cat, 'if you only walk long enough.'

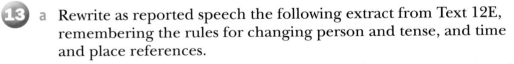

b Now replace each use of *said* in your answer with a different and more precise verb.

c Copy and complete the second line in each pair below to turn the direct speech into reported speech. Refer to the key point below to help you.

  i 'What is it?' they asked.
  They wanted to know . . .

  ii The Cheshire Cat enquired of Alice, 'Where are you going?'
  The Cheshire Cat enquired of Alice . . .

  iii 'Do you have a ticket to the match?' he queried.
  He queried . . .

Key point

Word order for reported questions

When a question beginning with a question word, e.g. *who, what, where*, is changed from direct to indirect/reported speech, there is an additional change, which is to the word order. Because direct speech uses the inverted subject/verb order necessary for asking questions in English, this becomes normal word order when the question is no longer being asked directly. No question mark is required in the reported speech version. Where the original question does not have a question word (as in example iii above), then *if* or *whether* is used to introduce the indirect question.

Text 12F on the next page is the opening of a story containing nonsense language called 'The Beginning of the Armadillos'.

 a On a copy of Text 12F, underline all the unusual words and expressions, and explain the effect of each of them.

b Find examples of repetition, alliteration and assonance, and explain the effect of these three devices in the passage.

c How many different ways of forming the future tense can you find in the passage? List them, and add to the list all the other ways you can think of.

Text 12F

This, O Best Beloved, is another story of the High and Far-Off Times. In the very middle of those times was a Stickly-Prickly Hedgehog, and he lived on the banks of the **turbid** Amazon, eating shelly snails and things. And he had a friend, a Slow-Solid Tortoise, who lived on the banks of the turbid Amazon, eating green lettuces and things. And so *that* was all right, Best Beloved. Do you see?

But also, and at the same time, in those High and Far-Off Times, there was a Painted Jaguar, and he lived on the banks of the turbid Amazon too; and he ate everything that he could catch. When he could not catch deer or monkeys he would eat frogs and beetles; and when he could not catch frogs and beetles he went to his Mother Jaguar, and she told him how to eat hedgehogs and tortoises.

She said to him ever so many times, graciously waving her tail, 'My son, when you find a Hedgehog you must drop him into the water and then he will uncoil, and when you catch a Tortoise you must scoop him out of his shell with your paw.' And so that was all right, Best Beloved.

One beautiful night on the banks of the turbid Amazon, Painted Jaguar found Stickly-Prickly Hedgehog and Slow-and-Solid Tortoise sitting under the trunk of a fallen tree. They could not run away, and so Stickly-Prickly curled himself up into a ball, because he was a Hedgehog, and Slow-and-Solid Tortoise drew in his head and feet into his shell as far as they would go, because he was a Tortoise; and so that was all right, Best Beloved. Do you see?

'Now attend to me,' said Painted Jaguar, 'because this is very important. My mother said that when I meet a Hedgehog I am to drop him into the water and then he will uncoil, and when I meet a Tortoise I am to scoop him out of his shell with my paw. Now which of you is Hedgehog and which is Tortoise? because, to save my spots, I can't tell.'

Rudyard Kipling

turbid	muddy

Key point

Forming the future tense

In English there are many different ways of indicating the future tense. There are three in the passage:

- present tense after *when* ('when you find')
- future auxiliary plus infinitive without *to* ('he will uncoil')
- present tense of the verb *to be* plus infinitive with *to* ('I am to drop').

The other ways are:

- *going to* plus verb (e.g. 'she is going to start piano lessons')
- *about to* plus verb (e.g. 'she is about to start piano lessons')
- present continuous (e.g. 'she is starting piano lessons').

Which form of the future is used depends partly on how soon the future event is likely to be, and how strong the intention is. The second and third of the options above, *will* and *am to*, are more definite in intention but less definite in time than the fourth and fifth options, *going to* and *about to*, which are normally used to show that something may happen in the near future. The use of the last option, the present continuous form, shows that something will definitely happen, and the time is often specified.

Text 12G

The Naming of Cats

The Naming of Cats is a difficult matter,
    It isn't just one of your holiday games;
You may think at first I'm as mad as a hatter
When I tell you, a cat must have THREE DIFFERENT NAMES.
First of all, there's the name that the family use daily,
    Such as Peter, Augustus, Alonzo or James,
Such as Victor or Jonathan, George or Bill Bailey –
    All of them sensible everyday names.
There are fancier names if you think they sound sweeter,
    Some for the gentlemen, some for the dames:
Such as Plato, Admetus, Electra, Demeter –
    But all of them sensible everyday names.
But I tell you, a cat needs a name that's particular,
    A name that's peculiar, and more dignified,
Else how can he keep up his tail perpendicular,

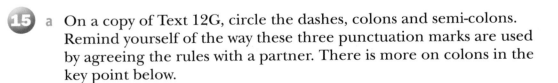

Or spread out his whiskers, or cherish his pride?
Of names of this kind, I can give you a quorum,
    Such as Munkustrap, Quaxo, or Coricopat,
Such as Bombalurina, or else Jellylorum –
    Names that never belong to more than one cat.
But above and beyond there's still one name left over,
    And that is the name that you never will guess;
The name that no human research can discover –
    But THE CAT HIMSELF KNOWS, and will never confess.
When you notice a cat in profound meditation,
    The reason, I tell you, is always the same:
His mind is engaged in a rapt contemplation
    Of the thought, of the thought, of the thought of his name:
His deep and inscrutable singular Name.

T.S. Eliot

15   **a**   On a copy of Text 12G, circle the dashes, colons and semi-colons. Remind yourself of the way these three punctuation marks are used by agreeing the rules with a partner. There is more on colons in the key point below.

Key point

Colons

Colons are quite rare. You learnt in Unit 8 that they are used in lists. They can also be used to introduce speeches, examples, or further explanations instead of the expression 'that is to say'.

b Explain the irony of the 'sensible everyday names' which are mentioned in Text 12G.

c Think of some male and female cat names which are:
- 'sensible'
- 'fancier'
- 'peculiar'.

16 a With a partner, discuss the eleven aspects of the poem in Text 12G listed below. First copy out the table so that you can make notes of your comments and collect examples of each aspect.

Aspect	Comment	Example
voice		
persona		
register		
audience		
form		
rhyme		
rhythm		
metre		
capitalisation		
vocabulary		
nonsense words		

b Prepare, practise and deliver a shared presentation on the poem to the class.

c Listen to the other presentations and prepare some constructive responses to give as feedback.

17 If creatures from another world landed on Earth they would probably consider many of the things and actions they observed to be nonsensical to them.

a In a group, discuss and make a list of buildings, objects and activities which might seem senseless from their viewpoint (e.g. an ice rink, a parking meter, a game of football).

b Draft a series of descriptions of the observations which they might report on when they go back to their own world: for example, 'Humans travel around in metal boxes on wheels which often line up and cannot move for a long time'.

c Recite your list of descriptions to the class. The class has to guess what you are referring to.

Acknowledgements

The authors and publishers acknowledge the following sources of copyright material and are grateful for the permissions granted. While every effort has been made, it has not always been possible to identify the sources of all the material used, or to trace all copyright holders. If any omissions are brought to our notice, we will be happy to include the appropriate acknowledgements on reprinting.

p. 5 from *The Lord of the Rings* by J.R.R. Tolkien. Reprinted by permission of HarperCollins Publishers Ltd, The Lord of the Rings © Fourth Age Limited 1954, 1955, 1966; p. 8 'Eureka! Archimedes' secret death ray is brought to light' by Jonathan Leake, Sunday Times, May 2000 © NI Syndication; p. 24 from *ZLATA'S DIARY: A CHILD'S LIFE IN SARAJEVO* by Zlata Filipović, translated by Christina Pribichevich-Zoric (Viking 1994, first published in France as 'Le Journal de Zlata' by Fixot et editions Robert Laffont 1993) Copyright © Fixot et éditions Robert Laffont, 1993. Reproduced by permission of Penguin Books Ltd and Viking Penguin, a division of Penguin Group (USA) Inc; p. 25 adapted from 'Rafa takes Spain home; clinches fifth Davis Cup' by Maha Mansoor, Khelo Pakistan, December 2011; pp. 32 and 176 'The Sea' and 'The Snitterjipe' by James Reeves © James Reeves from *COMPLETE POEMS FOR CHILDREN* (Heinemann); p. 33 'The Bay' by James K. Baxter from *Collected Poems*; p. 36 adapted from 'A Drink of Water' from *Ways of Sunlight* by Samuel Selvon, used with permission; p. 58 'Puducherry on top' by Manju Malhi for Open Skies, September 2009, used with permission of the author; p. 60 from the blog www.antoniotahhan.com, adapted and used by permission of Antonio Tahhan; p. 64 from *Long Walk to Freedom* by Nelson Mandela, published by Little, Brown Book Group, copyright © 1994 by Nelson Rolihlala Mandela. By permission of Little, Brown and Company. All rights reserved; p. 68 Excerpt from *CHINESE CINDERELLA* by Adeline Yen Mah. Reproduced by permission of Penguin Books Ltd. Copyright © 1999 by Adeline Yen Mah. Used by permission of Delacorte Press, an imprint of Random House Children's Books, a division of Random House, Inc. Any third party use of this material, outside of this publication, is prohibited. Interested parties must apply directly to Random House, Inc for permission; p. 71 'Amish barn raising' by Harvey McGavin from the TES, 8 June 2001; p. 73 'My secret life as a teen detective' interview by Clio Williams, Sunday Times Magazine, June 2010 © NI Syndication; p. 80 'Lightning Bolt gunning for 9.4 as sprint king vows to smash 100m world record in London', Daily Mail, April 2012 © Solo Syndication; p. 81 'Usain Bolt's Olympic 100m triumph triggers jubilation in Jamaica' by Kwesi Mugisa and Hugh Muir, Guardian, August 2012, Copyright Guardian News & Media Ltd 2012; p. 82 'Bolt's heartland of Sherwood Content erupts in celebration' Courtesy of Jamaica Observer Limited © 2012, Horace Hines - Staff Reporter; p. 84 adapted with permission from the short story 'Emotion of Speed' by Eileen Hughes, published June 2007 on www.helium.com; p. 89 from *A Game of Polo with a Headless Goat and Other Bizarre Ancient Sports Discovered in Asia* by Emma Levine, Andre Deutsch 2000; p. 99 'The Tortoise and the Hairpin: a tale of life in the slow lane' by Mark Cocker from Guardian Weekly magazine, June 2000, Copyright Guardian News & Media Ltd 2000; p. 104 'Friend' by Hone Tuwhare from *Small Holes in the Silence: Collected Works*, Godwit Press, Random House NZ, 2011, used by permission of the Estate of Hone Tuwhare honetuwharepoetry@gmail.com; p. 111 from *Wind, Sand and Stars* by Antoine de Saint-Exupéry © Gallimard, 1939; p. 118 from *Polar Dream* by Helen Thayer, with adaptations by permission of the author; p. 121 from *THINGS FALL APART* by Chinua Achebe (William Heinemann, 1958, Penguin Classics, 2001). © Chinua Achebe 1958. Reproduced by permission of Penguin Books and The Wylie Agency (UK) Limited; p. 129 from *AS I WALKED OUT ONE MIDSUMMER MORNING* by Laurie Lee (Penguin Books, 1971) © Laurie Lee 1969. Published and reproduced by permission of Penguin Books Ltd and Andre Deutsch; p. 132 South African Great Karoo text used with permission; p. 133 Grenada advert text used by permission of Virgin Holidays; p. 139 from *Picnic at Hanging Rock* by Joan Lindsay, published by Chatto & Windus, reprinted by permission of The Random House Group Limited; p. 144 "Little Sa' winds her way up to Lhasa' by Zheng Jinran in Beijing and Daqiong in Lhasa from China Daily, May 2012; p. 146 'Second Glance at a Jaguar' from *Wodwo* by Ted Hughes, reprinted by permission of Faber and Faber Ltd, and from *COLLECTED POEMS* by Ted Hughes, copyright © 2003 by the Estate of Ted Hughes. Reprinted by permission of Farrar, Straus and Giroux, LLC; p. 147 'Hunting Snake' by Judith Wright from *A Human Pattern: Selected Poems* (courtesy the publishers ETT Imprint, Sydney 2010); p. 150 by Lee Krystek from the Unnatural Museum www.unmuseum.org; p. 157 'Boli-mania hits the concert hall' by Paul Gent, Telegraph, April 2009, © Telegraph Media Group Limited 2009; p. 159 'Four-year-old piano prodigy to play Royal Albert Hall' by Anna Davis, Education Correspondent, London Evening Standard, April 2012, © Solo Syndication; p. 163 'Ballet gives me the biggest high' interview by Sue Fox, Sunday Times Magazine November 2009 © NI Syndication; p. 164 'Every Body Is Doing It' *Wicked World* by Benjamin Zephaniah (Puffin 2000). Text © Benjamin Zephaniah, 2000, illustrations © Sarah Symonds, 2000. Reproduced by permission of Penguin Books Ltd; p. 166 Adapted with permission from a review on www.fandango.com; p. 173 'Write-A-Rap Rap' by Tony Mitton from *A Handful of Poems* published by BritLit Kit, 2007, used with permission from David Higham Associates; p. 181 'The Naming of Cats' from *Old Possum's Book of Practical Cats* by T.S. Eliot, reprinted by permission of Faber and Faber Ltd

Thanks to the following for permission to reproduce copyright photographs:

Cover Thor Jorgen Udvang/Shutterstock; p. 1 Stock Connection Blue/Alamy; p. 2 Mary Evans Picture Library; p. 5 Jules Kitano/Shutterstock; p. 6 Rainer Ksobiak/Fotolia; p. 8 Burning Mirrors, Stanzino delle Matematiche, 1587–1609 (fresco), Parigi, Giulio (1571–1635) (attr. to)/Galleria degli Uffizi, Florence, Italy/The Bridgeman Art Library; p. 11 Chromographs/Shutterstock; p. 13 R. Gino Santa Maria/Shutterstock; p. 16 Israel Travel Photos – Jerusalem © Rafael Ben-Ari/Fotolia; p. 19 DKImages; p. 21 AFP/Getty Images; p. 24 REUTERS/Stringer; p. 26 AFP/Getty Images; p. 28 Martin Green/Fotolia; p. 29 (cricket) Inspirestock Inc./Alamy, (hockey) Richard Wareham Fotografie (Nieuws)/Alamy; p. 31 Dushenina/Shutterstock; p. 32 Nejron Photo/Shutterstock; p. 36 Condor 36/Shutterstock; p. 39 Three Images/Getty; p. 42 Alex Mustard/Naturepl.com; p. 43 Dave stamboulis/Alamy; p. 45 Thomas Barrat/Shutterstock; p. 47 Images & Stories/Alamy; p. 49 Jupiterimages/Thinkstock; p. 51 Michele Falzone/Alamy; p. 55 Andrew Jalbert/Shutterstock.com; p. 58 Neil McAllister/Alamy; p. 60 Infinity21/Shutterstock; p. 61 Imagebroker/Alamy; p. 64 Michele Falzone/Alamy; p. 66 AFP/Getty Images; p. 69 Anjum Gupta/Alamy; p. 70 Paul Prescott/Shutterstock.com; p. 71 Three Lions/Getty; p. 73 iStockphoto/Thinkstock; p. 76 (bus driver) Brand X Pictures/Thinkstock, (grocer) Fuse/Thinkstock, (traffic warden) Kenneth William Caleno/Shutterstock.com; p. 77 M. Rohana/Shutterstock.com; p. 80 AFP/Getty Images; p. 82 2012 Felix Kunze/Getty; p. 84 iStockphoto/Thinkstock; p. 86 Bob Daemmrich/Alamy; p. 88 Mary Evans Picture Library/CHARLES FOLKARD; p. 89 AFP/Getty Images; p. 95 Jose Ignacio Soto/Shutterstock.com; p. 97 The Art Archive/Alamy; p. 99 Xpixel/Shutterstock.com; p. 102 Photobank.kiev.ua/Shutterstock.com; p. 103 Nigel Hicks/Alamy;

Cambridge Checkpoint English 8